Association: Stepping-Stone or Alternative to EU Membership?

David Phinnemore

Copyright © 1999 Sheffield Academic Press

Published by
Sheffield Academic Press Ltd
Mansion House
19 Kingfield Road
Sheffield S11 9AS
England

Typeset by Sheffield Academic Press
and
Printed on acid-free paper in Great Britain
by Cromwell Press
Trowbridge, Wiltshire

British Library Cataloguing in Publication Data

A catalogue record for this book is available
from the British Library

ISBN 1-84127-000-8

Contents

Tables

Series Foreword

This is the sixth publication in the series Contemporary European Studies produced in collaboration between Sheffield Academic Press and the University Association for Contemporary European Studies (UACES).

UACES, the lead organization in bringing together academics and practitioners concerned with the study of contemporary Europe, celebrates its thirtieth anniversary in the year 2000. The main emphasis of the Association's work has been in the sphere of European integration and, in particular, the institutions and activities of the European Union. The dramatic and often turbulent developments in Europe since 1989 have posed new challenges to the European Union, and have greatly added to the excitement and complexity of the agenda of academic European studies. This series reflects those interests and is designed to meet the needs of those studying contemporary Europe by providing authoritative texts dealing with a wide range of issues, with the emphasis on the European Union. One of the intentions of the series is to include promising younger authors—as well as some more experienced hands—in the list of contributors.

Enlargement to bring in new members from post-Communist Central and Eastern Europe is now one of the key issues on the agenda of the European Union. This book, the latest addition to the Contemporary European Studies list, provides a timely assessment of the experience of association, the major form in which the European Community/ Union has sought to define its relations with neighbouring states. As David Phinnemore shows, the meaning and substance of this form of relationship have changed over time, and have been a source of some confusion and frustration for the parties involved. This has been particularly clear in the case of the latest 'Europe Agreements' involving the Central and Eastern European States. This book provides a clear, detached and informative survey of an area of the EU's practice that has been a mixed success and recently the subject of much critical comment.

In the production of this book, I am grateful to Jean Allen of Sheffield Academic Press for her continuing support for the series, and to Rebecca Cullen for her efficiency and enthusiasm; and not least, to the author for his good-humoured cooperation and meticulous observation of deadlines.

Judy Batt
Series Co-Editor

Acknowledgments

The preparation and writing of this book have involved the support of various individuals and institutions. In particular, I wish to thank Judy Batt of the University of Birmingham for her most helpful comments and advice on the text; Clive Church of the University of Kent for generating my interest in association and for his comments on the original draft; and my wife, Antonia, for her support and patience.

Abbreviations

APC	Association Parliamentary Committee
Bull. EC	*Bulletin of the European Communities*
Bull. EU	*Bulletin of the European Union*
CAP	Common Agricultural Policy
CCP	Common Commercial Policy
CEE	Central and Eastern European
CEE(6)	Bulgaria, the Czech Republic, Hungary, Poland, Romania and Slovakia
CEE(10)	CEE(6) plus Estonia, Latvia, Lithuania and Slovenia
CET	Common External Tariff
CFSP	Common Foreign and Security Policy
CMEA	Council for Mutual Economic Assistance
EC	European Community
EC(6)	Belgium, Federal Republic of Germany, France Italy, Luxembourg, Netherlands
EC(9)	EC(6) plus Denmark, Ireland, United Kingdom
EC(10)	EC(9) plus Greece
EU(12)	EC(10) plus Portugal and Spain
ECJ	European Court of Justice
ECR	*European Court Reports*
ECSC	European Coal and Steel Community
ECU	European Currency Unit
EEA	European Economic Area
EEC	European Economic Community
EFTA	European Free Trade Association
EIB	European Investment Bank
EP	European Parliament
EU	European Union
GATT	General Agreement on Tariffs and Trade
GDP	Gross Domestic Product
GDR	German Democratic Republic
GSP	General System of Preferences
IGC	Intergovernmental Conference
JHA	Justice and Home Affairs

JOCE	*Journal officiel des Communautés européennes*
JPC	Joint Parliamentary Committee
MECU	Million ECU
MEDA	Euro-Mediterranean Partnership
MEP	Members of the European Parliament
NATO	North Atlantic Treaty Organization
OEEC	Organization for European Economic Cooperation
OJ	*Official Journal of the European Communities*
PHARE	Pologne, Hongrie, Assistance à la Réconstruction Economique
PJCCM	Police and Judicial Cooperation in Criminal Matters
SEA	Single European Act
SPO	State Planning Organization (Turkey)
TAIEX	Technical Assistance Information Exchange Office
UK	United Kingdom
US	United States
USSR	Union of Soviet Socialist Republics
WEU	Western European Union
WTO	World Trade Organization

Introduction

The 1990s have been one of the busiest periods in the external relations of the European Community (EC) and the European Union (EU).[1] The revival of the EC in the late 1980s, the completion of the internal market and the introduction of a single currency have established the EU as the central organization in the European integration process. Occupying such a position has meant that the demand for closer ties and membership has been considerable. Following the launch of the '1992' project in the mid-1980s, states in Western Europe were eager to obtain access to the internal market of over 320 million people. The end of the Cold War only increased their keenness to avoid being marginalized from the mainstream of economic and political developments in Europe. The collapse of communism in Central and Eastern Europe (CEE) has also resulted in CEE states knocking on the EU's door for assistance with their reform processes and their attempts to become fully involved in European integration. For many European states, the goal is membership of the EU.

Dealing with so many requests has not been easy for the EU. The advantages of closer ties—such as increased trade and increased security—are acknowledged. There is also great sympathy for the CEE states' desire to 'return to Europe'. Yet since its creation the EC has only had limited experience of developing closer relations with European non-Member States. Although ambitious association agreements were signed with Greece and Turkey in the 1960s, most relations established in the 1970 and 1980s, including the associations with

---

1.   In line with common academic usage, the term 'European Community' and the abbreviation 'EC' are only used for the period after 1967. When referring to the EC prior to this date, the term 'European Economic Community' and the abbreviation 'EEC' are used. For the period since November 1993, the term 'European Union' and the abbreviation 'EU' are used where reference is being made to the EU in general and not specifically to the EC as its first pillar.

Malta (1971) and Cyprus (1973), involved little more than free trade agreements covering industrial goods. How to respond to the demands from its European neighbours has been a major challenge for the EC/EU. The sheer number of European states seeking closer ties has been unprecedented. There is hardly a European state that has not made a request of some sort. Nearly all have sought improved market access and cooperation. Eighteen have applied for membership (see Table 1). The types of state seeking integration have varied too. Not only is the EC/EU having to develop relations with states possessing highly developed economies, it is also having to deal with the totally new situations presented by CEE states: the EC had no experience before 1989 of developing ties with and integrating former command economies. Even more of a challenge for the EC/EU has been how to balance the development of closer relations and ultimately the accession of new members with a deepening of its own integration. Having undergone a revival in the late 1980s, the EC/EU has had no desire to see the renewed dynamic stifled by the interests of non-Member States and the need to accommodate new members.

Table 1: Membership Applications

Country	Date	Country	Date
Greece	12.06.1975	Poland	05.04.1994
Turkey	14.04.1987	Romania	22.06.1995
Austria	17.07.1989	Slovakia	22.06.1995
Malta	16.07.1990	Latvia	13.10.1995
Cyprus	04.07.1990	Estonia	24.11.1995
Sweden	01.07.1991	Lithuania	08.12.1995
Finland	18.03.1992	Bulgaria	14.12.1995
Switzerland	26.05.1992	Czech Republic	17.01.1996
Norway	25.11.1992	Slovenia	10.06.1996
Hungary	31.03.1994		

The response to these challenges has been to revive association as a form of external relations. Only rarely used on previous occasions in a European context, the flexibility of association has proved attractive to the EC/EU in the 1990s (see Appendix 1). Three existing associations—those with Turkey, Malta and Cyprus—have been either revitalized or upgraded, and two new types of association created. The first is the so-called 'European Economic Area' (EEA) with Austria, Finland, Iceland, Liechtenstein, Norway and Sweden, all advanced industrial economies of the European Free Trade Association (EFTA).

The second new type of association is the Europe Agreement. This has been devised for CEE states with agreements so far being concluded with Bulgaria, the Czech Republic, Estonia, Hungary, Latvia, Lithuania, Poland, Romania, Slovakia and Slovenia. As a result of these developments, the number of EC associates in Europe has risen from three in 1989 to 16 today (see Table 2). Association has become a central element of EC/EU external relations in the 1990s.

Table 2: Association Agreements

Country	Signed	In force
Greece	09.07.1961	01.11.1962*
Turkey	12.09.1963	01.12.1964
Malta	05.12.1970	01.04.1971
Cyprus	19.12.1972	01.06.1973
Hungary	16.12.1991	01.02.1994
Poland	16.12.1991	01.02.1994
Czechoslovakia	16.12.1991	—
Austria	02.05.1992	01.01.1994*
Finland	02.05.1992	01.01.1994*
Iceland	02.05.1992	01.01.1994
Liechtenstein	02.05.1992	01.05.1995
Norway	02.05.1992	01.01.1994
Sweden	02.05.1992	01.01.1994*
Switzerland	02.05.1992	—
Romania	01.02.1993	01.02.1995
Bulgaria	08.03.1993	01.02.1995
Czech Republic	04.10.1993	01.02.1995
Slovakia	04.10.1993	01.02.1995
Estonia	12.06.1995	01.02.1998
Latvia	12.06.1995	01.02.1998
Lithuania	12.06.1995	01.02.1998
Slovenia	10.06.1996	01.02.1999

* Lapsed on state's accession to the EC/EU.

For the EC/EU the main purpose of each association is the development of closer ties with the associate. Association provides a mechanism through which cooperation in numerous areas can be pursued. It can be used to provide access to EC markets and involve other European countries in EU policies and programmes. Most associates, however, tend to view association as involving more than simply cooperation. Association is very much seen as a stepping-stone to membership. In fact almost every one of the EC's current associates has applied for membership. In some cases, the fact that association is being viewed as a stepping-stone to membership is made clear even before the association is established. Five states have submitted applications prior to their association being established. A further four have applied on or before signing their association agreement (see Appendix 2). In other cases, experiences of association have helped push states into applying for EC/EU membership. For the majority of European states that enter into associations, the relationship is seen as a stepping-stone rather than as an alternative to EU membership.

The fact that only a few associates have become members of the EU does raise doubts as to whether association should be viewed as a stepping-stone to membership. Certainly the European Economic Community (EEC) initially viewed association as a mechanism that could help states to become members. In the 1960s, associations were explicitly designed with this goal in mind. The EEC was wary about establishing associations with states not intent on membership, fearing that these might compromise the EEC's own integration efforts. Since then, however, the EC has developed into a much more robust and dynamic organization, keen on deepening its own integration. It has therefore shown a reluctance to admit new members fearing that a larger membership might slow down the deepening process. Concerted efforts have been made to avoid any direct link between association and accession. This change in attitude led to association being viewed more as an alternative to membership. That the EC/EU position has shifted and that such views are at variance with those of associates emphasizes the ambiguity of association and the fact that its purpose is open to various interpretations. It also underlines the flexibility of association. With the EC/EU in the 1990s being faced with so many requests for ties, it is hardly surprising that it should have turned to association as the mechanism with which to respond. If association can provide the basis for wide-ranging cooperation and satisfy the interests of states keen on integration while not ruling out the possibility of membership, its attraction to the EC/EU is clear.

Outline of the Book

The purpose of this book is essentially threefold. First, it introduces association and provides an overview of the different agreements concluded by the EC with European states.[2] Secondly, the book seeks to establish the nature of association and determine whether it can provide an acceptable alternative to accession. A final purpose is to assess the contribution that associations past and present have made to an associate's prospects for accession to the EU. In other words, is association a stepping-stone to EU membership?

The focus of the first chapter is the flexibility of association. The chapter begins by examining the contents of Article 238 (310) of the 1957 Treaty of Rome which state that an association shall involve 'reciprocal rights and obligations, common action and special procedures'.[3] It is in these limited and vague provisions that the flexibility of association lies. As the discussion shows, association may take various forms, ranging from little more than a free trade agreement to a relationship that falls only marginally short of membership. Equally, the purpose of individual associations may vary. The ambiguity means that for states unwilling to subscribe fully to the EC's goals and activities, association can be used to establish a high degree of cooperation. Alternatively, an association may be regarded as an evolving relationship involving a state which, owing to particular economic or political circumstances, is not in a position to assume the obligations of EC/EU membership. Indeed, the express purpose of an association can be to facilitate the eventual membership of the associate. Such considerations are followed by a brief overview of how association agreements are concluded. This is important since the content and purpose of any association will be determined by those who negotiate and approve the agreement. The chapter's final section picks up on the ambiguity of association and establishes the various principles which the EC has adopted in using Article 238 (310). For the most part, these have never been formally stated. The EC and its Member States have been keen to ensure that the flexibility of association remains. Yet certain conditions governing a state's eligibility for association have been laid down.

2.   As noted below (p. 25), association is technically with the EC. Despite calls from the European Parliament (Hänsch 1992: 24) for relevant treaty amendments to be introduced, there is no provision for association with the EU.

3.   The Treaty of Amsterdam in 1997 renumbered the vast majority of articles in the Treaty of Rome (Treaty establishing the European Community). Here the text uses the original and more familiar numbering, placing the new article numbers in parentheses immediately after.

The flexibility of association also features in the second chapter. This concentrates on the various forms that association may take by examining the various association agreements the EC has concluded with European states. The analysis focuses on five areas: the aims of association, possible trade bases, levels of cooperation, the institutional frameworks envisaged, and the question of eventual EC/EU membership. The first two agreements considered are the so-called 'Athens Agreement', which the EEC signed with Greece in 1961, and the 'Ankara Agreement' signed in 1963 with Turkey. With both states regarded at the time as being insufficiently economically developed to join the EEC, the associations were conceived as interim arrangements which could later lead to membership. The second two agreements are those with Malta (1971) and Cyprus (1973). These are much more limited in contents and aim. They were also the last agreements to be signed for almost two decades. The next associations were not established until 1994. The first of these was the EEA, the most advanced form of association to date, albeit not one designed to lead to EU membership. The next associations were those created by the Europe Agreements with CEE states.[4] Although drawn up to meet the latter's aspirations to 'return to Europe', the Europe Agreements were not conceived as stepping-stones to membership.

Having examined the different forms of association, the book's third chapter analyses associates' experiences of the relationship. These are dealt with under eight headings. The first three deal with the establishment of the associations, the maintaining of the relationship, and the functioning of the institutional framework. The next set focuses on the impact of association on relations in terms of trade, the levels of financial assistance granted, and the scope and content of the cooperation developed as a consequence of the relationship. The final two sections deal with the development of associations once established, first as an evolving relationship per se, and secondly as a stepping-stone to membership. What emerges is that experiences of association have been mixed. Rarely has the relationship established functioned to the satisfaction of all concerned. The flexibility of association has, how-

---

4.   These Europe Agreements were the first association agreements to be signed with former socialist states in Europe. In 1983, the EC did sign a Cooperation Agreement with the then Socialist Federal Republic of Yugoslavia which was concluded on the basis of Article 238 (310). At no point was the relationship referred to as an association.

ever, enabled a shift in the purpose of some associations. In the majority of cases, associations have been reoriented towards the attainment of EU membership.

The purpose of the fourth chapter is to draw together the lessons of associations to date and to assess their implications. The chapter's first section provides an overall assessment of association as a flexible form of relationship with the EC. A second section then examines the role of association as an alternative to membership with attention being drawn to its limitations created by the de facto satellization that associates experience. The third section focuses on the position and value of associations in the process of EC/EU enlargement. The key question addressed is whether association can and should be viewed as a stepping-stone to membership. The final two sections assess the prospects for those associations that currently exist and the possibility of further associations being established.

The conclusions drawn in the book certainly suggest that association can provide an alternative to EU membership. Yet whether association is an acceptable alternative to membership must be doubted. The EU has few reservations about states remaining associates. For associates, however, the attractions of the relationship as an alternative to membership are limited. The absence from decision-making means that associates assume the status of de facto satellites of the EU. For many states the effect is to make membership more attractive. Association is viewed very much as a stepping-stone to membership. However, stepping-stones are only stepping-stones if they actually lead to the desired destination. Membership does not automatically follow from association. An associate may accede to the EU, but accession will only take place if the EU decides to admit the associate concerned. Association in itself does not guarantee membership.

1 |

Association, Flexibility and the Principles of Practice

A major attraction of association for both the EC/EU and non-Member States is its flexibility. Associations can take different forms and be put to various uses according to the needs and interests of the EC/EU and would-be associate. This flexibility stems from the vague provisions of the Treaty of Rome. The key article, Article 238 (310), offers only a brief definition of association. It involves 'reciprocal rights and obligations, common action and special procedures'. Nothing more specific is said. The actual content and purpose of the association is left open. Analysis of the relevant provisions in the Treaty of Rome can, however, provide an indication of what may be involved. Hence, the first section of this chapter takes a look at Article 238 (310) and other treaty provisions to establish some basic features of association. The section also underlines its flexibility. The fact that the content of an association is not predetermined by the Treaty of Rome means that much is left to the negotiations towards an agreement. The chapter's second section therefore takes a brief look at how association agreements are concluded. This allows the key actors in determining the content of associations to be identified. The final section of the chapter then explores the debates which have taken place since 1957 surrounding the purpose and content of association. In doing so, it identifies the various principles that have governed the use of association at different points. It also draws attention to the various prerequisites that states have to meet before they can become associates.

Treaty Provisions on Association

The legal basis for all association agreements established by the EC with European states is contained in Article 238 (310) of the Treaty of

Rome.[1] Back in 1957 when the Treaty was signed, the Article consisted
of three paragraphs. The first of these stated:

> The Community may conclude with a third State, a union of States or an
> international organization agreements establishing an association involving
> reciprocal rights and obligations, common action and special procedures.

This was later amended by the Maastricht Treaty in 1992. The reference
to 'a union of States' was replaced by a more wieldy and appropriate
reference to 'one or more states'. Consequently, the Article now reads:

> The Community may conclude with one or more States or international
> organizations agreements establishing an association involving recipro-
> cal rights and obligations, common action and special procedures.

A further amendment introduced by the Maastricht Treaty was to move
the second and third paragraphs to Article 228 (300). These concerned
the conclusion of agreements (see below).

What remains in Article 238 (310) therefore is a rather vague
description of what association involves: reciprocal rights and obligations, common action and special procedures. The fact that the description is vague was intentional. At the time when the Treaty of Rome was
signed the six signatories were keen to ensure that flexible provisions
for external relations existed. This would facilitate the establishment of
ties with various states interested in a formal relationship. Notable
among potential partners were the other industrialized states of western
Europe including the United Kingdom. In 1956, the Organization for
European Economic Cooperation (OEEC) had begun talks on the
establishment of a European free trade area and the Six were keen to
ensure that provision was included in the Treaty of Rome for the conclusion of such an arrangement. Indeed, Article 238 (310) was written
with the OEEC talks in mind. Its existence also reflected a desire on the
part of the Six to ensure that suitable links could be established with
less-developed European states. Turkey, for example, had already
expressed an interest in the EEC. Finally, the Six were committed to the
establishment of associations with various African and South-American
states.[2] Association was clearly going to be used for different purposes.

1.   Other provisions governing association appear in Part Four of the Treaty of
Rome. This contains Articles 131-136a (182-188) and is concerned with the
association of overseas countries and territories.
2.   When the Treaty of Rome was signed, declarations of intent regarding the
establishment of associations with Morocco, Tunisia, Libya, Italian Somalia,

The relevant Treaty provisions could not be too prescriptive.

The vagueness of Article 238 (310) does not mean that an understanding of association cannot be established. Awareness of the provisions in the Treaty of Rome does reveal some basic features of an association. Moreover, if the provisions of Article 238 (310) are compared to others governing the external relations of the EC, a first indication of what association entails can be gained. Indeed, the fact that association agreements are concluded by unanimous vote in the Council implies that they involve more than simply trade. Trade agreements are based on Article 113 (133) of the Treaty of Rome and require only a qualified majority. Also, given that there are no geographical constraints on which states may become associates, association involves less than EC or EU membership. According to what was originally contained in Article 237 of the Treaty of Rome and now appears in Article O (49) of the Maastricht Treaty (see Appendix 3), membership is restricted to European states. Association must therefore fall somewhere between the two, a view widely voiced during the early years of the EEC. For example, the Commission President, Walter Hallstein, maintained on several occasions that association can be anything between full membership minus 1% and a trade and cooperation agreement plus 1%. Such a view has been borne out by practice. In the hierarchy of the EC's contractual relations with non-member countries, association involves more than a trade agreement yet falls short of membership. This has also been inferred by the rulings of the European Court of Justice (ECJ). In its 1987 *Demirel* ruling,[3] reference was made to the 'special privileged links with a non-member country' created by an association. While avoiding any statement on the substance of association, the observation clearly suggested that the relationship involves more than just a formal trade agreement.

Returning to the wording of Article 238 (310), this can be used to create a reasonably coherent picture of what is meant by association. A first point is that the phrase 'establishing an association' implies a degree of permanency to the relationship. Associations are assumed to involve a durable if not permanent link. Practice has shown this to be true. All association agreements to date have either been concluded for an unlimited period or contained a provision for renewal in advance of their expiry. The sense of commitment implied by permanency is also

Surinam and The Netherland Antilles were adopted.
   3.   *Case 12/86, Demirel v. Stadt Schwäbisch Gmünd, ECR* 1987: 3719-55.

evident in the fact that, under Article 228(7) (300(7)) of the Treaty of
Rome, associations like other external agreements are 'binding on the
institutions of the Community and on Member States'.

With regard to 'reciprocal rights', the presence and prominence of
such a requirement in an association causes little surprise. Reciprocity,
after all, is required under international law and no state is likely to
enter into an arrangement with the EC unless reciprocity exists. That
said, there is nothing in Article 238 (310) to say that reciprocity must
be strictly adhered to. Nor is there any requirement that it should be
complete. Association can therefore involve a broad balance of rights
and obligations. Equally, reciprocity need not be immediate. In an association, rights and obligations may be assumed over time and on an
asymmetrical basis, particularly where the EC wishes to take into
account the associate's comparative economic strength and its ability to
meet obligations. The flexibility in association which this implies is,
however, constrained by the EC's commitment with regard to international trade. Participation in the General Agreement on Tariffs and
Trade (GATT) and, since 1995, the World Trade Organization (WTO)
means that the EC cannot grant an associate unilateral trade preferences
unless they are also extended to all other GATT/WTO members.
Exemptions are, however, possible. Unilateral preferences may be
granted under Article 24(5) GATT provided that they lead to the
'formation of a customs union or a free trade area'.[4] Any customs union
or free trade area must cover 'substantially all the trade between the
constituent territories' (Article 8(8) GATT) and must include 'a plan
and schedule for the formation of such a customs union or of such a
free-trade area within a reasonable length of time' (Article 5(5)(c)
GATT). The notion of 'reasonable' has been interpreted as being normally no more than ten years.[5] Hence, where an association with the EC
involves trade matters, it must entail the creation, possibly on an
asymmetrical basis, of either a customs union or a free trade area within
a period of ten years.

The second key element of association is 'common action'. What this
should cover is not clear. It is to be expected, however, that any common action will be in line with the EC's objectives. This was implicit in

4.   General Agreement on Tariffs and Trade, 30 October 1947 (via
http://www.wto.org).
5.   Understanding on the Interpretation of Article XXIV of the General Agreement of Tariffs and Trade 1994 (via http://www.wto.org).

the ECJ's *Demirel* ruling in 1987 when it stated that an associate 'must, at least to a certain extent, take part in the Community system'. An earlier ECJ ruling on the EC's treaty-making power is also helpful in providing an indication of the what any common action may cover. In *AETR*,[6] the ECJ established the principle of *parallelism*, stating that:

> The Community enjoys the capacity to establish contractual links with third countries over the whole field of objectives defined by the Treaty. This authority arises not only from an express conferment by the Treaty, but may equally flow from other provisions of the Treaty and from measures adopted, within the framework of those provisions, by the Community institutions.[7]

The ECJ later reaffirmed and expanded on the principle in *Kramer*,[8] stating that the EC's authority to enter into international commitments arises:

> not only from an express conferment by the Treaty, but may equally flow *implicitly* from other provisions of the Treaty, from the Act of Accession and from measures adopted within the framework of those provisions, by the Community institutions.

The implication of *parallelism* for association is clear: common action may cover any areas where the EC has either an explicit or implicit internal competence to act. An association may therefore involve common action in areas as diverse as the environment, consumer protection and transport. It is worth noting that over time the areas of potential common action have increased as the EC has evolved. This is reflected in the content of recently concluded agreements compared to those signed in the 1960s. There are, however, limits. Since association is with the EC and not the EU, any association concluded cannot legally include common action in areas covered by the EU's two intergovernmental pillars. Although a pure EC association can involve a wide variety of areas of common action, it cannot deal with either the Common Foreign and Security Policy (CFSP) or what was, prior to the Treaty of Amsterdam, Justice and Home Affairs (JHA) and is now Police and Judicial Cooperation in Criminal Matters (PJCCM). As shown in the discussion of 'mixed' agreements below, however, there are ways in

6.   *Case 22/70, Commission v. Council (AETR), ECR* 1971: 263-95.
7.   For a discussion of the *AETR* judgment and the subsequent development of the EC's treaty-making powers, see McGoldrick (1997: 48-61).
8.   *Joined Cases 3, 4 and 6/76, Kramer and Others, ECR* 1976: 1297-1328.

which it is possible to ensure that associations do involve matters beyond the competences of the EC. The scope of common action could be limitless.

Indeed, if, as was certainly the original intention with the Athens and Ankara Agreements, the purpose of the association is to facilitate the accession of an associate to the EC/EU, then there is little reason to limit the common action. Not all areas of EC activity may initially be covered, but if the association is designed to lead to membership then the coverage can be extended over time. Alternatively, where the association is not designed to lead to membership, then the extent of the common action may vary. Much will depend here on whether the EC believes its interests will be best served by pursuing cooperation. Common action can clearly be wide-ranging, evolving, variable and possibly aimed at facilitating the associate's later accession to the EC/EU.

What form common action should take is not made explicit in the treaty provisions. The reference to 'action' does, however, suggest more than simply consultation. Indeed, where an association is to be based on a customs union, it is to be expected that at least coordinated if not common commercial and economic policies should be included. The harmonization of legislation in key areas of economic activity can also be envisaged. In fact, such a requirement is commonplace.

The third element of association noted in Article 238 (310) is 'special procedures'. The reference is widely accepted as implying the establishment of an institutional framework for both the implementation of the association agreement's provisions and the furtherance of the common aims of the EC and the associate. It is also accepted that the 'special procedures' should be unique to the association. Early in the 1960s Greek voices were heard calling for associates to be involved in the EEC's internal institutional and decision-making structures. The Six quickly agreed, however, that participation in these was the preserve of Member States alone. Allowing associates access to decision-making could threaten the EC's decision-making autonomy and act as a brake on their own integration efforts. As a result, each association is equipped with its own institutional framework.

This often consists of institutions comparable to those in the EC: an association council made up of representatives from the Council and the associated state's government; an association committee of Commission officials and senior civil servants from the associated state; and a parliamentary association committee with parliamentarians from the European Parliament (EP) and the associated state. Other institutions may also be established (see p. 58). There are limitations, however. The ECJ, in its Opinion 1/91 concerning the European Economic Area Agreement, stated that Article 238 (310) does not provide any basis for setting up a system of courts that conflicts with the provisions of the Treaty of Rome. The proposed EEA Court had to be abandoned.

Clearly, associations can take various forms. They may involve the creation of either a free trade area or a customs union. This may be achieved asymmetrically and over a lengthy period of time. Common action may cover few or many areas of mutual interest provided that they fall within the EC's treaty-making power. Hence, an association could be minimalist and involve little more than free trade with the possibility of some cooperation at a later date. Alternatively, it could involve a more enhanced economic relationship based on a customs unions with cooperation extending into all areas of EC activity. With the expansion in EC competences since 1958, common action today could extend as far as participation in economic and monetary union.

The scope of association would appear, however, to be limited by the EC's treaty-making power. Yet opportunities exist to overcome any such constraint. Two points should be noted. The first concerns a provision originally contained in Article 238 (310) and currently found in Article 228 (300) (see Appendix 3). It allows for the Treaty of Rome to be amended to enable the conclusion of an association agreement. Obviously, those who drafted the Treaty of Rome did not wish to rule out the possibility that associations would involve matters beyond the EC's competences. Hence, the scope of an association with the EC appears to be limitless, provided Member States are willing to amend the Treaty of Rome accordingly. The existence of a provision does not mean, however, that it will necessarily be used. In fact, no amendment has ever been made to the Treaty of Rome to enable the conclusion of an association agreement. All the same, associations dealing with matters beyond those covered by the EC's treaty-making powers have been established. This leads to the second point: the possibility of concluding so-called 'mixed' agreements. These are termed 'mixed' because they are signed by both the EC and its Member States. Adopting such an approach means that agreements may cover areas beyond those for which the EC is competent and deal with areas where the Member States retain treaty-making power (McGoldrick 1997: 78-

88). This is particularly important now that the EU has been established. The availability of 'mixed' agreements means that CFSP and JHA matters can be covered by associations. It also means that potential scope of association is well beyond that already available under the flexible provisions of Article 238 (310).

The Conclusion of Association Agreements

In theory, the flexibility of association appears to be limitless. Even if the EC's treaty-making powers restrict the content of pure associations with the EC, the use of a mixed agreement can ensure that additional areas are covered. With no clear legal limit on what association may involve, the actual nature and scope of any association agreement will therefore be determined by the actors involved in its conclusion. These are not difficult to identify. The procedure by which association agreements are concluded is relatively straightforward.[9] It is found in Article 228 (300) (see Appendix 3).

The first step towards the conclusion of an association agreement is the opening of negotiations. This takes place once the EC's negotiator, the Commission, has received a negotiating mandate from the Council. The Commission then undertakes negotiations with the would-be associate. The negotiations are carried out 'in consultation with special committees appointed by the Council' and with the Commission referring back to the Council whenever an extension or modification of its mandate is necessary. Once negotiations have been completed, the agreement is initialled by the chief negotiators and then, once checked and translated, signed. In the case of pure association agreements, the signing ceremony involves the Presidency of the Council and the competent representative of the associate-to-be. 'Mixed' agreements are also signed by a competent representative from each of the EC's Member States. Once signed, the agreement must be ratified by each of the signatories. With pure association agreements, this requires, on the EC side, the assent, since 1987, of the European Parliament. 'Mixed' agreements also need to be ratified in line with the constitutional requirements of each of the Member States. Once this has taken place,

---

9.   Indeed, the original second paragraph of Article 238 (310) stated that 'agreements shall be concluded by the Council, acting unanimously after consulting the Assembly'. Since the Maastricht Treaty, the provisions have been amended and expanded and moved to Article 228 (300).

the agreement is formally concluded by the Council acting unanimously. Establishment of the association then takes place normally within two months.

Clearly, from this brief outline of procedure, the Council is the key institution on the EC side. Not only does it issue the mandate for negotiations and watch over the Commission as it negotiates, the Council is also responsible for concluding the agreement. Hence, the Member States are highly influential. This reflects the fact that the unanimity requirement provides each of them with the power to veto any proposed association. It also enables each of the Member States to have a direct influence on the scope and timing of any agreement. Various negotiations confirm this. A recent example can be found in the delays brought about by certain Member States in the negotiations towards the first Europe Agreements in 1990–91. On one notable occasion the French brought negotiations to a halt when they refused to accept proposals for an increase of 500 tons in annual beef imports. An example from an earlier set of negotiations is the Italian veto which led the EC's negotiations with Austria to collapse in 1967. If such influence for the Member States was not enough, where an association agreement is 'mixed', it also extends down to national parliaments as the main institutions involved in ratification. Evidently, the Member States and the Council are the key players in the conclusion of association agreements.

Other institutions do have a role. The Commission normally provides a draft negotiating mandate for Council approval and indeed carries out the negotiations. As noted, its room for manoeuvre is limited. The European Parliament is also involved in the conclusion of an agreement. Originally it was only consulted but since the Single European Act (SEA) it has been required to give its assent to any agreement. In effect, therefore, although the European Parliament is not involved in the actual negotiation of association agreements, it does have a veto over their conclusion.[10] This applies not just to agreements but also to additional and supplementary protocols. Were the Commission or the Council to ignore the comments of the European Parliament during the negotiation of an agreement, the possibility of assent being withheld could not be ruled out. Indeed, the European Parliament has rejected measures put to it under Article 238 (310).

10. Under the 1973 Luns-Westerterp procedure, the EP is kept informed of progress in negotiations and informed of their outcome before any association agreement is formally signed.

A fourth EC institution that can be involved in the conclusion of an association agreement is the ECJ. Under Article 228 (300), the Council, the Commission or a Member State may obtain, prior to conclusion of an agreement, the opinion of the ECJ as to the compatibility of the proposed agreement with the Treaty of Rome. Where the opinion is negative, the agreement as it stands may only be concluded after appropriate amendments to the Treaty of Rome. To date, the referral of an association agreement to the ECJ has taken place on only two occasions, both concerning the EEA Agreement. The first of these was in 1991 and saw the proposed agreement rejected, thus confirming the Court's power. The agreement was subsequently amended and re-presented to the Court in 1992. On this occasion, the ECJ approved the agreement.

The Principles of Practice

The manner in which association agreements are concluded clearly provides the Member States with a key role in determining the vagueness of Treaty provisions governing association. This does not mean, however, that the use of association and the contents of agreements have been left exclusively to the Member States to decide. Other institutions have been influential. In particular, the Commission and the European Parliament have been key actors in setting out a series of principles concerning association. These have never been written down in a dedicated document. Rather, they have emerged at various points in the history of the EC, notably during the first 15 years. They constitute what might be referred to as the principles of practice.

The first attempts at developing an approach to the use of association were made immediately prior to and in the first few years after the creation of the EEC. This reflected the desire of the Six to move towards a European free trade area, often referred to as a European economic association, with other OEEC states. An Interim Committee established to coordinate the position of the Six noted in 1957 that association should involve more than just a free trade area. The coordination or harmonization of competition policies would have to be included (Lindberg 1963: 141-42). The following year in October 1958, the so-called 'Okrent Report' was published. This represented the view of the Six and argued that an association—in this case one with the other members of the OEEC—'must not in any way prejudice either the content or the implementation of the Treaty of Rome'. Priority would be given to safeguarding the EEC's treaty base and ensuring that the integration envisaged therein would not be compromised. All associates would have to accept the EEC as an evolving entity. They could not expect the EEC to restrict its own development for the sake of concluding an association agreement. The report also reiterated the views of the Interim Committee by arguing that an association would have to involve not just a free trade area but also the coordination of trade policies, the convergence of economic and financial policies, the harmonization of social conditions, legislative approximation, and the free movement of workers. Such a position contributed to the collapse of the OEEC talks since commitments along the lines stated would have been unacceptable to other OEEC states. The views did, however, enjoy support within the Commission. They were evident in both its first annual report and its so-called 'First Memorandum' published in February 1959. This also drew attention to the flexibility of association and emphasized the fact that the associate would retain 'full individuality on the political plane' (EEC Commission 1959: 87). This implied non-participation in EEC institutions.

So, during the first two years of the EEC's existence, some basic principles began to emerge regarding the use and content of association: first, no association should impede integration within the EEC; secondly, association should not involve simply a free trade area, but entail policy coordination if not harmonization; and thirdly, involvement of the associate in the EEC's internal decision-making processes was not on offer. Each of these emerging principles was to be evident in the structure and content of the first two association agreements, those concluded with Greece and Turkey in 1961 and 1963 respectively (see Chapter 2). They would also be evident in some of the early reports of the European Parliament and in the reaction of the Commission to the prospect of associations being established with neutral states following the UK application for EEC membership in 1961.

Although the role of the European Parliament in the early development of the EEC was generally limited, its views on association were certainly influential. The Birkelbach report drawn up in 1960–61 by the European Parliament's Political Committee is a case in point, being welcomed within the Commission and certainly not rejected by any of the Member States. Its basic argument was that the norm for European states should be EEC membership and not association. Association with countries unable or unwilling to become members contained various dangers and in creating associations, the EEC would run the risk of undermining its capacity to survive and develop. Association with European states was not, however, ruled out. All the same, it would have to involve more than a customs union and cover other policy areas, in particular competition policy, the adoption of the CET, and 'a whole series of provisions relating to economic union'. An equal say in the EEC's decision-making processes could not, however, be guaranteed. Such an arrangement would therefore only appeal to those wishing ultimately to become members.

Viewing association as a precursor or stepping-stone to membership was certainly popular at this time. The only two association agreements concluded in the 1960s with European states—those with Greece and Turkey—both had membership as a strategic objective of the association (see below, p. 63). The link between association and membership was never confirmed. However, unofficially at least, it was for some an unwritten half-principle governing the use of association. Only those states intent on membership should be allowed to become associates.

Such a restrictive view was not universally accepted. In 1963, a second report from the European Parliament, the Blaisse Report, argued that association was possible 'for countries which, though unable or disinclined to join the Community, are nevertheless prepared to play their part in the integration process by harmonising their economy with that of the Community to a really appreciable extent'. Hence, provided they were willing to accept a significant level of integration—the report referred to a customs union with common policies in some areas—states not wishing to join the EEC could become associates. A similar position was adopted by the Commission's External Relations Department. In a report on the neutral states' applications for association in 1961, it acknowledged that association would not necessarily have to lead to membership (EEC Commission 1962). Indeed, it was assumed that 'association [could be] considered as a permanent solution, rather than with a view to subsequent development into full membership'. Nevertheless, any association would have to involve both 'close and permanent links...embodied in special institutions' and wide-ranging economic cooperation. Furthermore, there was a clear desire for any association to involve at least partial harmonization. On the question of decision-making, the report re-emphasized earlier statements stressing that participation in the EEC's institutions was the 'exclusive privilege of the member countries'. The report also sought to use association in a way which would not allow it to threaten the EEC's own internal integration. It therefore proposed a two-stage agreement with the neutrals which would allow the EEC to develop its own policies before progressing with the association.

Although the Birkelbach and Blaisse reports were clearly read with interest within the EEC, neither they nor the unpublished internal report of the Commission constituted an official policy. Indeed, Commission officials acknowledged that association had yet to be defined and that the EEC wished to remain flexible in its use of Article 238 (310). Moreover, there were clear differences of opinion as to whether association should be reserved exclusively for those states which were seeking a stepping-stone to membership or whether it should be made freely available as a long-term, if not permanent, alternative. Nevertheless, questions were being asked in Brussels concerning the appropriateness of the existing pragmatic step-by-step approach towards association. Given that the trade concessions contained in the Athens and Ankara agreements would have a greater commercial impact on Italy, it was not surprising that the Rome government was keenest to establish an association policy.

In a memorandum of its own on association submitted to the Council on 4 May 1964, the Italians made their case for a policy which in many respects was more restrictive than that proposed by Birkelbach.[11] Indeed, it appeared to offer little scope for using association as the basis for relations with European countries. First, it was argued that it was impossible to create a permanent association with a European country since such an arrangement would allow the associate to enjoy the benefits of the common market without assuming appropriate responsibilities. Any association should therefore be seen as a step, via a customs union and ultimately an economic union, towards membership.[12] Secondly, it was argued that an association should only be concluded with a democratic state. And thirdly, the Memorandum proposed compensating those Member States (e.g. Italy) most affected in trade terms by the creation of associations.

The response to the Italian Memorandum was generally negative, and for two reasons. First, the Memorandum spoilt the idea of the EEC

11. See 'A propos du mémorandum italien', *Revue du marché commun* 69 (1964): 213-16.

12. The Italians were willing to treat Austria, which at the time was seeking association, as an exception (Plessow 1967: 184).

Community having an 'open' character. Secondly, the adoption of a rigid set of principles would undermine the flexibility available in the conduct of external relations. In some quarters, it was even suggested that acceptance of the proposals would paralyse the EEC's external relations (Ungerer 1964: 695). On these points Italy's five partners seemed united: the French were keen to see negotiations opened with Spain; the Germans were eager to have Austria associated with the EEC as soon as possible; and the Benelux countries wanted to keep all options for enlargement open. For its part, the Commission was still keen not to rule out association as a means for European states to *rejoindre* the EEC. Also, the absence of a single policy was in the interests of the individual Member States. It not only provided each of them with a valuable bargaining chip in relations with any country applying for association, it also ensured that they would not be tied to any policy (Rey 1963: 58). The power to veto would therefore not be compromised. The third reservation concerned the proposed compensation. The general view was that this was contrary to the spirit of the Treaty of Rome and would be difficult to evaluate. Moreover, any disadvantages to a southern Member State might be counterbalanced at a later date or more immediately by an enlargement to the north.

Given the reservations expressed by Italy's partners no real progress towards the development of either a set of principles or a coherent policy governing association was made during the mid-1960s. Instead, the Six remained content to deal with applications for association on a pragmatic case-by-case basis. They were also eager to retain the advantages created by the flexibility of Article 238 (310). Nevertheless, the existence of the Italian Memorandum alongside the European Parliament and Commission reports did increase awareness of the perceived drawbacks involved in creating associations. Hence, they reinforced an increasingly popular yet unofficial view that association should be restricted to those countries with less developed economies intent on using the relationship as a transitional stage or stepping-stone towards membership. Association was not automatically viewed as appropriate for those EFTA states keen on remaining outside an enlarged EEC. All the same, there was a desire to retain the flexibility implicit in the provisions of Article 238 (310).

Such a point of view was reflected in a third European Parliament report issued in 1967. The Dehousse Report touched on two issues: the conditions for, and the economic content of, an association. In doing so, it challenged Birkelbach's contention that membership should be the norm for European states and questioned whether candidates for association and accession should have to meet the same political conditions. Thus, while stating that association should not be made available to countries with 'an avowedly anti-democratic system of government' (e.g. Spain), the report argued that it would be 'inadvisable to be too inflexible' regarding the political conditions for association generally. In addition, Dehousse advocated a pragmatic approach to the question of association, pointing out that the vague provisions of Article 238 (310) served such an approach well. As regards the economic content of an association, the report proposed that a customs union with 'some features of an economic union' would be most appropriate.

Dehousse's advocacy of a more flexible approach towards association coincided with the Commission making its views on association clearer. First, Robert Toulemon, Director of the Directorate General for External Relations, argued that the possibility of enlargement required due consideration of the future of association (Toulemon 1967). Most of his comments appeared, however, to be designed to ward off potential associates. Having noted that, in principle, association should be regarded as a preparatory stage towards membership, Toulemon questioned whether, given the level of integration required in an association, it would be in the interests of a European state to accept EC policies in the formulation of which, owing to its exclusion from EC decision-making procedures, it played no role. As for the EC, he warned against a multiplication of associations for practical as well as political reasons. Servicing a large number of associations would certainly act as a drain on EC resources. Evidently, fears still existed that associations could retard the EC's own progress.

Such reservations concerning the use of Article 238 (310) were also apparent in the Commission's 1967 opinion on enlargement. In this, the Commission reaffirmed that membership was the most appropriate arrangement for European democracies with advanced economies. Nevertheless, it did acknowledge that association could be made available to European states whose level of development precluded membership, provided, however, they had 'free' institutions. Evidence of the EC's commitment to this proviso had already been shown. Following a coup d'état and the overthrow of democracy in Greece in early 1967, its association with the EC was effectively frozen. For the next seven years, it would function simply at the level of *gestion courante* (current administration) (see p. 76). The EC appeared serious in insisting on a state being democratic as a prerequisite for association.

The Commission's view that membership should be the norm for European states essentially restated previous restrictive interpretations on the use of association. However, the opinion did show a degree of flexibility with regard to the neutrals. While arguing that a preferential agreement (i.e. an association) with a developed country not intent on eventual membership would raise problems, it was stated that association could be made available to countries that, as a result of their international situation, were prevented from joining the EEC. Clearly a reference to Austria and Finland, the loose wording was, according to reliable sources, also designed to cover Sweden and Switzerland. It was stressed, however, that in establishing any association, the EC would have to take 'every possible precaution in order to safeguard the complete independence of its decisions and to avoid unduly complicating the harmonious working of the customs union'. Indeed, on decision-making, potential associates were warned that 'in certain cases' they would have to 'conform with decisions in the taking of which they had no part'. Once again, the EC's emphasis was on giving priority to its own integration. Moreover, the EC was intent on retaining its decision-making autonomy.

Such views were also reflected in a second Commission opinion on enlargement (EC Commission 1968). Yet this contained no explicit reference to association even as a mechanism that could facilitate the ultimate accession of those countries seeking membership. The attraction of association appeared to be evaporating, a view shared by the Member States. Indeed, various aide-memoires, proposals and declarations issued by the Member States in 1968, and on which the Commission's opinion was based, failed to refer explicitly to either association or Article 238 (310).[13] So too did the communiqué issued by the Hague Summit of EC leaders in 1969. It simply referred to 'special links' (*Bull. EC* 1-69: 4). The Commission's subsequent opinion on the position of EFTA states which had not applied for membership also failed to mention association (EC Commission 1971). And, when it came to discussing what arrangements should be established with those EFTA states not involved in the first enlargement of the EC in 1973, associa-

---

13. The proposals, declarations and aide-memoires are reproduced in *Bull. EC* 3-68: 17-22 and *Bull. EC* 5-68: 10-13.

tion hardly featured. The preference was for trade agreements based on Article 113 (133). Certain EFTA states such as Sweden and Portugal were keen on association, but the EC's position was clear. The Council, meeting in November 1970 with representatives of those EFTA states not seeking EC membership, declared that the EC was not willing to enter any arrangement which 'would interfere with the enlarged Community's autonomous decision-making powers, its common policies, its smooth functioning and its prospects for further development' (cited in EC Commission 1971: 3). A wide-ranging association as an alternative to membership was not on offer.

So, by the time of the EC's first enlargement in 1973, no official policy on or set of principles for the use of association in a European context had been officially formulated. This undoubtedly reflected a desire to retain as much flexibility as possible in terms both of what an association could contain and the purposes to which association could be put. That said, there appeared to be an implicit understanding that any association with a European state should entail wide-ranging cooperation and be viewed as an arrangement which could in time lead to membership. Hence, any would-be associate would have to be democratic. Moreover, nothing in the association should be allowed to impede the development of the EC. Given such views, the fact that the 1960s saw only limited use of association in a European context should come as no surprise. Only two associations, those with Greece and Turkey, were established. The limited enthusiasm for association was also reflected in the fact that only two additional association agreements were signed with European States in the 1970s. Of note too is the fact that these agreements with Malta and Cyprus were essentially minimalist in their content and aims (see Chapter 2).

This limited enthusiasm for association at the time of the EC's first enlargement remained in place for at least the next 15 years. No more associations were established and no real efforts were made to utilize Article 238 (310) in a European context. Moreover, no states sought association. In part, this reflected the fact that the EFTA states now had free trade with the EC and were generally satisfied with promoting any cooperation on an ad hoc basis. Indeed, even when the EC emerged from the eurosclerosis of the 1970s and became a more dynamic organization in the 1980s, none of the EFTA states openly advocated association as a desirable form of relations with the EC. Government reports on European integration either ignored association as a policy option or expressed little enthusiasm. Even those European states that did want either to establish closer relations or to move beyond existing relations with the EC saw little attraction in association. They opted instead for membership. Once Greece, Portugal and Spain emerged from dictatorship in the 1970s each immediately sought accession. The Commission did express a preference for association prior to membership, but the Member States opted to open accession negotiations believing that membership would help consolidate reforms in the three states. Even for economically less advanced countries, association was no longer being viewed, as once it might have been, as a desirable stepping-stone to membership.

The apparent disinterest in association did not, however, last. By the late 1980s, thought was being given, following the decision of the EC to embark on the completion of the internal market, to an upgrading of relations between the EC and the EFTA states. Also, from late 1989 onwards, attention was being given to how the EC should respond to the calls from Central and Eastern European (CEE) countries for close ties in the wake of the collapse of communism in Central and Eastern Europe. In both cases, the EC opted for association. In part, the EC was responding to the requests for closer ties. Yet its proactiveness also reflected a desire to ensure that priority could be given to its own integration. Every effort was being made to avoid any widening of the EC that might compromise its renewed deepening. When reviving association, the EC also began setting out explicitly the principles that would govern the development of ties with European countries. Many of them reflected concerns raised in the 1960s. While the principles would be applicable to the use of association, they would not predetermine the content of associations. Its flexibility would thus remain intact.

The first set of principles was laid down in 1987 when the Commission set out its position on the future of EC–EFTA relations. In what were referred to as the Interlaken Principles, the Commission declared that in developing any closer relationship with the EFTA states, the EC would be giving priority to its own internal integration. The second principle announced that the autonomy of the EC's decision-making processes should not be threatened, and third, the Commission declared that a fair balance be achieved between benefits and obligations (*Bull. EC* 5-87: 2.2.14). In terms of their content, the principles broke no new ground. Each had previously surfaced in earlier statements regarding association. What was new, however, was that the points were being formally declared as principles governing the EC's external relations, and by implication its use of association. What had previously been implicit regarding the use of association was now explicit.

The same point can be made, at least in part, with regard to a second set of principles. These emerged from the Commission's proposals for Europe Agreements with the CEE countries. Here, the Commission made the conclusion of such agreements conditional on would-be associates 'giving practical evidence of their commitment to the rule of law, respect for human rights, the establishment of multi-party systems, free and fair elections and economic liberalization with a view to introducing market economies' (EC Commission 1990a: 2). By implication, association would only be established with a democratic state with a market-based economy. The conditionality was emphasized in the Europe Agreements. Early agreements include references in their preambles, while agreements signed after 1992 contain so-called 'democracy clauses' requiring respect for democratic principles, human rights and the principles of the market economy. Reference is also made to respect for minority rights. A key, yet hitherto unwritten, principle governing the use of association was being made explicit: only democratic states were eligible. This was later emphasized when the Maastricht Treaty inserted Article 228a (301) into the Treaty of Rome. This provides for the interruption or suspension of relations with non-Member States where such action is provided for in a common position or joint action adopted within the framework of the CFSP.

The Commission's proposals on the Europe Agreements certainly appear to reiterate earlier principles, but they deviate in one crucial respect from the earlier justification for insisting that an associate was a democracy. In the 1960s Franco's Spain was deemed ineligible for association on the grounds that such a relationship was viewed as a stepping-stone to membership. In the case of the CEE countries, however, Europe Agreements were being proposed as sui generis agreements and not as pre-accession arrangements. They would have 'a special value in themselves...[which] should be distinguished from the possibility of accession to the Community' (EC Commission 1990a: 2). Although future accession was not being ruled out, the link between association and membership was no longer being acknowledged. Wary that an increased membership could jeopardize its own integration and reluctant to extend what may be seen as a promise of membership, association was presented as a sui generis arrangement. Association was no longer being viewed as a stepping-stone to membership.

Summary

The key point that emerges from the discussion in this chapter is the flexibility of association. The vagueness of Article 238 (310) coupled with the treaty-making powers of the EC and the possibilities created by mixed agreements enable the EC to conclude far-reaching and wide-ranging association agreements. Where appropriate, these may result in relationships that provide stepping-stones to EC membership. A further point to emerge is that the EC has been slow to develop a clear set of principles governing the use and purpose of association. At different points in the development of the EC, views on the desired content and long-term objectives of associations have changed. Consequently, different forms of association have emerged. It is these that provide the focus of the next chapter.

2 |

Forms of Association

The flexibility of association provides the EC with an exceptionally useful mechanism for the conduct of its external relations. Association can be put to various uses to develop relationships with non-Member States which reflect the specific needs and interests of both parties. This has made it particularly attractive since the mid-1980s as the EC/EU has responded to requests for closer ties from numerous quarters including Central and Eastern Europe, the EFTA states and existing Mediterranean associates. The view that association has various possible uses is not, however, new. Early on in the development of the EC, the flexibility of association was recognized. Association could be used to create little more than a free trade area. Alternatively, a wide-ranging association could be established involving levels of cooperation and integration that would place the associate in a position only marginally short of actual membership. Indeed, the purpose of an association might be to prepare a state for later accession to the EC/EU. All this was acknowledged in early analyses of association. The relationship was viewed as one that could involve either limited cooperation, where the associate does not intend to accede to the EC, or a more dynamic relationship leading to membership. Since then, associations have taken other forms and served different purposes. This not only underlines the flexibility of association but also the fact that perceptions of its possible use have changed.

This chapter analyses the main features of the various association agreements concluded by the EC and highlights the major similarities and differences between them.[1] Attention is focused first on the aims, objectives and rationales of each association. Common features do exist, although the more economically developed an associate, the more ambitious the association generally is. A second feature examined is the

1.   All the agreements have been published in the *OJ*. See Appendix 1 for details.

trade regime envisaged. Here, there are three basic forms of association: customs union-based (Greece, Turkey, Cyprus); free trade area-based (Malta, Cyprus, Europe Agreements); internal market-based (EEA). Third, the chapter looks at the scope and level of cooperation and commitments envisaged as part of an association. Some associations are essentially minimalist (Malta and Cyprus) while others involve numerous commitments and areas of cooperation (e.g. the EEA and Europe Agreements). A fourth feature of association is the institutional framework established by each association agreement. A high degree of similarity between associations is revealed, although different levels of contact and involvement with the EC do exist depending on the extent of cooperation and integration envisaged. Finally, associations are compared in terms of their long-term purpose. In some cases, association may be viewed as a permanent relationship. In others, the express purpose may be to prepare the associate for eventual accession to the EC/EU. Thus, association appears capable of being both an alternative and stepping-stone to membership.

The Aims, Objectives and Rationales of Association

The various association agreements signed by the EC, albeit with a few exceptions, each have their own specific aims, objectives and rationales.[2] In general, these are determined by the associate's state of economic development. Similarities do, however, exist. A first concerns the promotion of trade. Not only do the agreements with Greece and Turkey aim 'to promote the continuous and balanced strengthening of trade and economic relations between the Parties', but so too does the EEA agreement. As for the agreements with Malta and Cyprus, they aim 'progressively to eliminate obstacles as regards the main body of trade between the [EC] and [Malta/Cyprus]'. The Europe Agreements, meanwhile, refer to promoting 'the expansion of trade and the [*sic*] harmonious economic relations'.[3] They also aim to establish or develop a free trade area covering substantially all trade.

2.   The exceptions are the Maltese and Cypriot agreements signed in the early 1970s and the Czech and Slovak Europe Agreements signed in 1993. In the case of both pairs of agreements, the aims are identical.

3.   Such an aim does not appear in Hungary's Europe Agreement but is implied in the reference to 'establish a free trade area...covering substantially all trade'.

A second similarity is that each association is viewed as an evolving relationship. This is not just in terms of trade, but also in terms of co-operation. Indeed, in some cases, the evolution of the relationship is seen to entail the associate achieving EC/EU membership (see pp. 62-69). This is certainly true of the Greek and Turkish agreements. Their preambles refer to the 'joint pursuit' of the ideals underlying the EEC and the establishment of 'ever closer bonds' between the people of the EEC and Greece and Turkey respectively. The perceived dynamism of the relationship was emphasized at the signing of Turkey's association agreement when the Commission President, Walter Hallstein, stated that the association was 'imbued with the concept of evolution' (cited in Vali 1971: 335). As for the EEA, this too is created on the under-standing that the relationship will evolve. Hence, the preamble refers to the aim of providing a 'harmonious development' of the EEA. This is supported by one of the agreement's objectives: 'closer cooperation' in fields other than the free movement of goods, services, capital and people. The Europe Agreements, too, are concerned with more than trade promotion. They refer to 'the development of close political rela-tions' and the associate's 'integration into the Community'.[4] Equivalent statements, however, are not to be found in the more minimalist agreements signed with Malta and Cyprus. Nevertheless, the fact that both contain statements envisaging negotiations towards a customs union clearly suggest that the associations would evolve.

Beyond trade promotion and the notion of association as an evolving relationship, there are no other aims, objectives or rationales which all agreements explicitly share. This is due to several factors: first, agree-ments are signed with states whose interests in establishing associations with the EC differ; secondly, the EC's interests in given associations may not be the same; and thirdly, differences in associates' levels of economic development preclude certain aims, at least at the outset of the association. Hence, the EEA with the economically-advanced EFTA states is the only association that has as its central aim the creation of 'a homogenous European Economic Area' involving 'equal conditions of competition' and 'respect of the same rules'. By contrast, a key aim of the agreements with Greece and Turkey is the economic development of the associates. The signatories express their resolve to

4.   Reflecting the fact that they were concluded after the Maastricht Treaty entered into force, the Europe Agreements with Estonia, Latvia, Lithuania and Slovenia refer to 'integration into the European Union'.

ensure the 'continuous improvement in living conditions' via 'accelerated economic progress and the harmonious expansion of trade', and
note the special problems presented by the development of the associates' economies. Indeed, in the case of the Ankara Agreement, the
preamble also recognizes the need to grant economic aid to Turkey.

No such aim is made explicit in the agreements with Malta and
Cyprus, but it is in the Europe Agreements. Hence, the associations are,
depending on the individual wording of agreements, either to 'support
[the associate's] efforts to develop its economy' or 'foster... dynamic
economic development and prosperity' in the associated state.[5] However, the rationale behind the Europe Agreement goes further in so far
as the associations are designed to assist with the processes of
economic and political transition which CEE countries have been
undergoing since 1989–90. The various agreements therefore aim to
support the efforts of the associate 'to complete the conversion to a
market economy' (Hungary, Bulgaria, Romania, Latvia, Lithuania and
Slovenia), 'make progress towards realizing...economic freedoms on
which the EC is based' (Hungary), and 'consolidate...democracy'
(Romania). The aims are also reflected in preambles that confirm the
'EC's willingness to provide decisive support for the implementation of
reform and to help [the associate] cope with the economic and social
consequences of structural readjustment' (Poland, Czech Republic,
Slovakia, Romania and Slovenia).

This brief discussion of the aims and objectives of different association agreements reveals a first set of differences between associations
(see Table 2.1). All share the aim of trade promotion and all are conceived either explicitly or implicitly as evolving relationships. That
said, whereas the Maltese and Cypriot agreements limit themselves to
these goals, the early agreements with Greece and Turkey go further in
envisaging assistance with the economic development of the associates.
Such aims are also explicit in the Europe Agreements, but here,
reflecting the recent economic and political experiences of the CEE
countries, the emphasis is on systemic reform and structural
readjustment. In contrast to all these agreements stands the EEA
Agreement. Its more ambitious aim of an homogenous EEA highlights
the fact that association can be used to create exceptionally close ties
with states that have advanced economies.

5.   In Romania's Europe Agreement, the reference to 'economic development'
does not include the words 'dynamic'. There is also no reference to 'prosperity'.

Table 2.1: Associations according to Aims, Objectives and Rationales

	Greece/ Turkey	Cyprus/ Malta	EEA	Europe Agreements
Trade promotion	*	*	*	*
Evolving relationship	*	*	*	*
Economic assistance	*			*
Adjustment assistance				*
Homogenous EEA			*	

Customs Unions, Free Trade Areas and the Internal Market

Associations also differ according to the type of trade regime that each association agreement sets out to create. Here, the EC is constrained by international rules governing trade agreements as laid down in the General Agreement on Tariffs and Trade (GATT) and by the World Trade Organization (WTO). These require that any unilateral trade preferences granted to an associate must lead to the establishment, within a reasonable period of time, of either a free trade area or a customs union covering substantially all trade (see p. 24). Hence, a key feature of all associations to date has been free trade in industrial goods. This involves the removal of all tariffs and quantitative restrictions on industrial trade between the EC and the associate. Some associations have gone further and envisaged not just free trade but also the establishment of a customs union. In such cases, associates have committed themselves to the adoption of the EC's Common External Tariff (CET) and the Common Commercial Policy (CCP). This more advanced trade regime has not, however, been integral to the most developed forms of association. While customs union did feature prominently in the early association agreements, later association agreements have all eschewed the idea. Instead, there has been a tendency to restrict the aims of the association to the creation of a free trade area for industrial goods.

The agreements with Greece and Turkey both saw the establishment of a customs union as an integral part of the association. In the case of Greece, a detailed timetable was provided which envisaged the customs union being established over 22 years and on an asymmetrical basis with the EC removing all tariffs and quotas at a faster rate than Greece.[6]

6.   The inclusion of a detailed timetable for the establishment of a customs union did not necessarily mean that the Agreement was compatible with GATT regulations. Indeed, GATT members did not explicitly support the Agreement. The

Whereas the EC was scheduled to provide Greek goods with free access to its market at a rate in line with the establishment of free trade within the EC, Greece would reduce all tariffs on imports of non-sensitive industrial goods from the EEC within 12 years. Tariffs and quotas on sensitive goods would be gradually reduced over the next ten years. By contrast, the agreement with Turkey simply envisaged the eventual establishment of a customs union 'within a reasonable period' after preparatory and transitional periods lasting a maximum of 23 years. The Ankara Agreement did not contain a detailed timetable for tariff reductions.[7] This reflected the need for greater flexibility in moving towards a customs union due to Turkey's relative economic weakness. An Additional Protocol was, however, signed in 1970 detailing the measures to be taken for the establishment of the customs union.[8] All tariffs and quotas governing trade between the EC and Turkey would be removed by 1995. Turkey was also committed to aligning itself to the CET and adapting its agricultural policy to the Common Agricultural Policy (CAP). The Additional Protocol was later supplemented by a customs union agreement signed in 1995.[9] Turkey's association with the EC, like Greece's before, was now clearly a *customs union association*.

The examples of Greece and Turkey suggest that the establishment of a customs union was initially seen as the ideal and preferred basis for any association between the EC and a European state. The view is supported not only by the EC's extreme reluctance early on to consider a simple industrial free trade area as the basis for a European Economic Association with the states of the Organization for European Economic Cooperation (OEEC) in the late 1950s, but also its insistence in the 1960s that any association with Austria be based on a de facto customs union. Yet, as the EC developed, the apparent centrality of a customs union to an association was challenged. This was due primarily to the difficulties experienced in moving towards customs union with Greece

EEC subsequently argued that, in the absence of an explicit rejection, the Agreement was not incompatible with GATT regulations (Flaesch-Mougin 1980: 226-27).

7.   Consequently, some countries were reluctant to accept the Ankara Agreement as compatible with Article 24 of GATT. However, pressure from the EEC and the USA for Greece and Turkey to be treated equally due to the position of Cyprus enabled the agreement to be approved (Tsalicoglou 1995: 31).

8.   *JOCE* L293, 29 décembre 1972.

9.   *OJ* L35/1, 13 February 1996.

and Turkey. In its place came an emphasis on free trade in industrial goods.

This decreasing emphasis on customs union can be detected in the second set of association agreements with European states: those concluded with Malta and Cyprus in the early 1970s. These envisaged the 'progressive elimination of obstacles to trade' and contained a less clear cut commitment to customs union. This does not mean, however, that the agreements envisaged no more than just a free trade area. They are not simply 'free trade associations'. Despite the absence of a timetable for the establishment of a customs union, both agreements do provide that the second stage will involve, in principle within five years, the adoption of the CET. Although no explicit reference is made to customs union, adopting the CET amounts to the de facto creation of such. In addition, the preamble to each agreement states that:

> eighteen months before the expiry of the first stage, negotiations *may* be opened with a view to determining the conditions under which a customs union between the Community and [Malta/Cyprus] *could* be established (emphasis added).

Critics of the agreements argue that this reference to customs union was simply inserted to enable conformity with GATT rules. This may be true. The fact remains though that customs union was certainly not ruled out. Indeed, both the Maltese and the Cypriot governments declared at the time the agreements were signed that they wished to see customs union established with the EC. Consequently, the relationships envisaged should be referred to as *potential customs union associations*. In the case of Cyprus, this potential was realized in 1987 when, following pressure from the Cypriot government, a protocol governing the establishment of a customs union by 2002 was signed.[10] Malta's association with the EC, however, has yet to move to the second stage. The first stage has simply been extended. Consequently, customs union is not envisaged.

The early emphasis on customs union did not feature in later association agreements. Instead, two new forms of association emerged. The first of these was created by the EEA Agreement. At one level, this represented a lesser form of economic integration since it fell short of a customs union. The EEA does not involve participating EFTA states adopting the CET. It does, however, involve the associates adopting the

---

10. *OJ* L393, 31 December 1987.

acquis communautaire governing the EC's internal market. In other words, the EEA requires the associated states to adopt the entire body of EC law governing the free movement of goods, services, capital and people. When the EEA Agreement was signed, this amounted to more than 1600 pieces of secondary EC legislation.[11] Moreover, participating EFTA states agree to adopt future additions and amendments. The EEA thus involves far more than simple tariff- and quota-free trade. It entails the removal of all non-tariff barriers to trade between the EC and the EEA associates. It thus creates a third basic form of association with European non-Member States: the *internal market association*.

Table 2.2: Associations and Trade Regimes

	Greece/ Turkey	Cyprus/ Malta	EEA	Europe Agreements
Free trade area	*	*	*	*
Customs union	*	*potential*		
Internal market			*	

The final form of association is the *free trade area association* created by the Europe Agreements with the CEE countries. This entails the removal of all restrictions on trade in industrial goods between the EC and its CEE associates. The Europe Agreements do not envisage free trade in agricultural goods. Nor do they envisage customs union. Two basic reasons explain this last point: first, a belief that the associates were insufficiently prepared technically to apply the relevant rules in full; and secondly, the argument that a customs union would have to cover agriculture, thereby necessitating an unwelcome overhaul of the CAP. Consequently, the Europe Agreements simply envisage the gradual and asymmetrical establishment of free trade in industrial goods over a period of normally ten years.[12] In terms of the trade regime they create, the associations with the CEE states appear to be the most limited to date. This does not mean, however, that they should be viewed as creating a lesser form of relationship than that found in earlier associations. As noted in the previous chapter, the flexibility of

11. Hence, the actual EEA Agreement in its 13 languages signed in Oporto on 2 May 1992 exceeded 15,000 pages in length and weighed approximately 100 kg.

12. The main exceptions to the ten-year norm are Lithuania, which negotiated a six-year transition period, Latvia and Slovenia, which negotiated a four-year transition period, and Estonia, which went immediately to free trade.

Article 238 (310) means that an association may involve much more than simply trade.

Cooperation and Commitments

In terms of the trade regime they create the Europe Agreements may appear limited. According to the additional commitments and the scope of cooperation envisaged, however, they create much closer relationships than those established by some of the earlier association agreements. For just as the trade regimes found in various association agreements differ, so too do the commitments laid down and the areas and extent of cooperation proposed. In some cases, cooperation is to be minimal. In others, it is planned to be extensive, often going beyond the competences of the EC thanks to the existence of 'mixed' agreements (see p. 27).[13]

At the minimalist end, two associations stand out: those with Malta and Cyprus. When signed, neither envisaged any form of economic cooperation or policy harmonization, at least not in the first stage. This situation changed. First, the EC concluded a series of financial protocols with both Malta and Cyprus from 1976 onwards (see p. 100). Secondly, in 1988, the EC–Cyprus association entered its second stage. During this, the principles governing competition, state aids and the approximation of legislation within the EC were also to be applied to the association. In addition, cooperation was due to be pursued in customs union-related matters. All the same, the commitments and scope of cooperation remained minimal.

The limited nature of the associations with Malta and Cyprus is somewhat surprising given what was envisaged in the first association agreement signed by Greece. This was, at the time, an essentially maximalist agreement that envisaged the promotion of 'joint measures' and policy harmonization covering agriculture, the free movement of workers, transport policy and competition. In addition, regular consultations would take place on the coordination of economic policies, with the treatment of exchange rate policy being treated as 'a matter of common concern'. Such provisions, alongside those relating to the freedom of establishment and the freedom to provide services, essentially

---

13. All association agreements concluded by the EC with European states, except those with Malta and Cyprus, have been 'mixed'.

mirrored those contained in the Treaty of Rome.[14] Hence, the association agreement with Greece has been described as both an 'EEC Treaty in simplified form' (Oppermann 1962: 504) and as a 'mini-Treaty of Rome' (Flaesch-Mougin 1980: 65). Also, the agreement contains a clause analogous to the catch-all Article 235 (308) of the Treaty of Rome. This provided for cooperation in any area necessary for the fulfilment of the association's objectives. The scope for cooperation therefore appeared to be considerable. Moreover, the agreement had attached to it a financial protocol committing the EEC to provide Greece with US$ 125 million of aid.[15] With the Athens Agreement, the EEC appeared to be testing the flexibility of association by pursuing a maximalist interpretation of what it might cover.

By contrast, although it contained a similar catch-all clause and had attached to it a financial protocol worth US$ 175 million, the association agreement with Turkey is far less ambitious. It makes no reference to either 'joint measures' or 'harmonization'. Rather, it simply states that the association will involve 'special rules' taking into account the EEC's common agricultural policy; entail 'closer coordination' of economic policies; be 'guided' by EEC Treaty provisions for removing restrictions to the free movement of workers, the freedom of establishment, and the freedom to provide services; lay down 'rules and conditions' for the extension to Turkey of the transport provisions in the Treaty of Rome; and involve an 'approximation' by Turkey of its rules on external trade with those of the EEC.[16] This looser wording clearly indicates the development of a weaker association. For Turkey, the looser wording also meant fewer obligations and, in the words of one Greek commentator, 'a painless association regime' (Roucounas 1964: 49). That said, with the entry into force of the 1970 Additional Protocol, the association was extended to involve the alignment of economic policies and the free movement of workers. Turkey was also obliged to

14. Compare Articles 4, 7, 12, 14, 16, 17, 22, 24, 29, 61, 70 of the EC–Greece association agreement with Articles 5, 9-10, 12, 14, 15, 17, 30, 32, 35, 106, 235 respectively of the Treaty of Rome before the Single European Act.

15. Indeed, it was very much due to the presence of the financial protocol that the agreement was mixed.

16. As far as competition, taxation and the approximation of laws are concerned, both agreements require that the principles in the Treaty of Rome 'be made applicable' to relations. In the case of the association agreement with Greece, detailed provisions to this end are included. No such provisions exist in the association agreement with Turkey.

adapt its agricultural policy to the CAP, albeit over a period of 22 years. The more recent 1995 agreement implementing the customs union involves the application of EC rules governing competition and state aid. It also increased the number of areas for possible cooperation.

So with the first four association agreements it concluded, the EC was able to envisage different levels of cooperation. As the agreements with Malta and Cyprus show, once the association with Greece had been established, there was a clear trend away from creating maximalist associations. Even the developments to the Cypriot and Turkish agreements in the 1970s and 1980s fall short of what was contained in the Athens Agreement. This trend would, however, be reversed in the 1990s when first the EEA agreement and secondly the Europe Agreements were signed. Both these envisage extensive cooperation between the EC and the associates. Moreover, in the case of the EEA, as the reference to the creation of a homogeneous European Economic Area implies, the commitments involved in the association are considerable.

Indeed, as far as the EEA is concerned, there is hardly an area of EC activity that is not covered. Not only does the EEA, as already noted, cover the *acquis communautaire* relating to the internal market, it also entails the EFTA associates adopting EC legislation in the so-called 'flanking areas' of social policy, consumer protection, the environment, statistics and company law. In several instances, the specific provisions of the EEA agreement mirror those in the Treaty of Rome prior to the amendments introduced by the Maastricht Treaty. Hence, the EFTA associates commit themselves to applying the principle of equal pay, promoting dialogue between management and workers at the European level, and pursuing EC objectives on the environment.[17] In addition, there are provisions promoting cooperation between the contracting parties in the following areas: research and development, information services, the environment, education, training and youth, social policy, consumer protection, small and medium-sized enterprises, tourism, the audio-visual sector and civil protection. Such cooperation may involve participation in EC programmes, joint initiatives, parallel legislation or coordination. If the scope of proposed cooperation were not enough, an evolutionary clause allowing the association to be extended to other areas not already covered is included. Added to this, the EEA Agree-

17. Compare Articles 66, 67(1), 69, 71, 73 and 75 of the EEA Agreement with Articles 117, 118a, 119, 118b, 130r(1-2) and 130t respectively of the Treaty of Rome before the Maastricht Treaty.

ment has attached to it a financial protocol designed to support the EC's efforts to reduce social and economic disparities within the internal market. Given that it is the EFTA states which fund the mechanism envisaged, the EC is essentially requiring payment for the privilege of participation in the EEA.

Without doubt, the EEA provides evidence of the flexibility of association and an apparent willingness to use this to the full. Indeed, considering the internal market basis of the association it creates, the EEA Agreement is without precedent in scope and content. Such a view is supported by EC officials. Armando Toledano Laredo, Director of the Commission's Legal Service in 1992, describes the Agreement as:

> the most formalized of all Community acts…the most advanced [association] agreement concluded hitherto…the most ambitious and the most complete agreement ever signed by the Community with a group of third countries (1992: 1201-1204).

On the EFTA side, Sven Norberg, Director of Legal Affairs in the EFTA Secretariat when the EEA Agreement was signed, argues that prior to the EU's 1995 enlargement, no Member State had assumed as many obligations and taken such large steps towards integration in one go as those EFTA states which became members of the EEA. He adds that 'it would hardly be possible to get any closer to the status of membership in the Community, without becoming a member, than through the present [EEA] Agreement' (1992: 1198).

Although the commitments envisaged may not be as numerous as in the EEA agreement, the scope of cooperation contained in the Europe Agreements is arguably as great. Indeed, in addition to general clauses on economic cooperation, industrial cooperation and cultural cooperation, each Europe Agreement provides for cooperation in more than 25 of the following areas:

- agriculture and the agro-industrial sector
- agro- and industrial standards and conformity assessment
- banking
- consumer protection
- customs
- drugs
- economics
- education and training
- energy

- environment
- fisheries
- housing and construction
- information and communication
- insurance
- investment promotion and protection
- monetary policy
- money laundering
- nuclear safety
- other financial services and auditing
- postal services and broadcasting
- prevention of illegal activities
- public administration
- regional development
- science and technology
- small and medium-sized enterprises
- social cooperation
- statistics
- telecommunications
- tourism
- transport
- water management.[18]

In addition, the agreements with Estonia, Latvia, Lithuania and Slovenia have a whole title dedicated to cooperation in the prevention of illegal activities. No agreement, however, contains an evolutionary clause. As for financial cooperation, although unlike the association agreements with Greece and Turkey in so far as no financial protocol is attached, the Europe Agreements do provide for assistance via the PHARE programme[19] and loans from the European Investment Bank.

A further feature of the Europe Agreements is the provision for political dialogue. For the most part, each states that the aim of the political dialogue is to 'accompany and consolidate' the rapprochement between the EC and the associate; 'to support the political and economic changes underway' in the CEE country concerned; and to 'contribute to the establishment of lasting links of solidarity and new forms

18. Not all agreements provide for cooperation in all areas listed. For example, cooperation in the area of housing and construction is only envisaged in the agreement with Lithuania.

19. Pologne, Hongrie, Assistance à la Réconstruction Economique.

of cooperation'. Political dialogue therefore covers matters both within and beyond the EC pillar of the EU. In particular, political dialogue is designed to involve cooperation in the context of the CFSP. Hence, the Europe Agreements refer to dialogue increasing the convergence of positions on international issues and enhancing security and stability in the whole of Europe. This makes the agreements unique. It would be wrong to conclude, however, that political dialogue takes place with only CEE associates. In fact, political dialogue was initiated with Cyprus and Malta in 1988, three years before the first Europe Agreements were signed. Later, in 1995, a scheme for regular political dialogue with Turkey was also agreed.

The scope of the cooperation and political dialogue envisaged with the EC's CEE associates suggests that the Europe Agreements are among the most wide-ranging association agreements signed by the EC. Such a view is reinforced when consideration is given to the fact that the CEE associates undertake to approximate their existing and future legislation with that of the EC. In each Europe Agreement, more than a dozen areas are explicitly mentioned. These include:

- banking law
- company accounts and taxes
- company law
- consumer protection including product liability
- customs law
- environment
- financial services
- food legislation
- indirect taxation protections of health and life of humans, animals and plants
- intellectual property
- protection of workers at the workplace
- rules on competition
- technical rules and standards
- transport.[20]

20. This list is based on the Europe Agreements with Hungary and Poland. Later agreements with Estonia, Latvia and Lithuania also refer to nuclear law, statistics, public procurement, and in the case of Latvia, labour law and entrepreneurial law.

Table 2.3: Associations, Cooperation and Commitments

	Greece	Turkey	Malta	Cyprus	EEA	Europe Agreements
Special rules	*	*				
Policy coordination	*	*				
Joint measures	*					
Approximation of laws	*	(*)		(*)	*	*
Policy harmonization	*					
Competition	*	(*)		(*)	*	*
State aid	*	(*)		(*)	*	*
CAP	*					
Free movement of workers	*	(*)			*	
Free movement of capital					*	
Free movement of services	(*)				*	
Flanking policies					*	
Cooperation	*	*		(*)	*	*
Evolutionary clause	*	*			*	
Financial protocol	*	*	(*)	(*)	*	
Financial cooperation			(*)	(*)		*
Political dialogue		(*)	(*)	(*)	(*)	*

Note: Parentheses indicate that the matter was not referred to in the original association agreement but results from either an additional protocol or another agreement.

In addition, each CEE associate is obliged to 'use its best endeavours to ensure that future legislation is compatible with Community legislation'. Later agreements with Estonia, Latvia, Lithuania and Slovenia also emphasize the importance of approximation of law to the association by calling for 'rapid progress...in the areas of the internal market, competition, protection of workers, environmental protection and consumer protection'.

Despite such provisions, the Europe Agreements are not as extensive as the EEA. This basically reflects the fact that the obligations of the EC and the CEE states are far fewer. Hence, although the free movement of capital and services is to be progressively established, the free movement of workers is limited to non-discrimination against existing legally-employed persons. Moreover, there is no legal obligation to adopt the *acquis communautaire* governing the internal market and the various flanking policies. That said, the CEE states are obliged, as are Turkey and Cyprus, to adhere to the Treaty of Rome's rules governing competition and state aid. And, as just noted, the Europe Agreements also oblige the CEE states to ensure that their domestic legislation is compatible with that of the EC. There are, however, no provisions governing policy harmonization.

Such a brief overview can only provide an indication of the commitments entered into and the cooperation envisaged in association agreements (see Table 2.3). It is clear, however, that associations can differ and that individual agreements can have their unique area(s) of cooperation or sets of commitments. Added to this, as the Cypriot and Turkish examples show, associations are not static. Over time commitments generally increase.

Institutional Frameworks and Decision-Making

A fourth area of interest concerns the institutional frameworks of associations and the position of associates vis-à-vis the EC's own decision-making procedures. Here, there are few major differences. Similar institutional frameworks have been established in each association. Also, no association involves participation in the EC's institutional arrangements. Hence, no associate has a decision-making role in any of the EC's own institutions. All the same, there are certain aspects of various institutional frameworks that differentiate associations.

The three institutions found in all associations to date are the asso-ciation council, the association committee, and the association parlia-mentary committee. The first of these, the association council, is the main political institution of the association. It consists of members of the Council of Ministers, the Commission and the government of the associate. In the case of the multilateral EEA Council, the number of government members from each associate is limited to one. Each asso-ciation council meets at least once a year and when circumstances require. Each also has a presidency that alternates between the EC and the associate every six months. The responsibilities of the association councils (with the exception of the EEA Council whose responsibilities are much fewer) cover five main areas. First, they are responsible for assessing or periodically reviewing the implementation of the association agreement and the overall functioning of the association. Secondly, they act as the main decision-making forum for the associa-tion. Decisions are adopted unanimously and are binding on all parties. A third function is to settle disputes. Fourthly, association councils are responsible for establishing, where necessary, committees and other bodies to assist them in carrying out their duties. Fifthly, those associa-tion councils established under Europe Agreements also have an explicit responsibility for discussing 'bilateral and international issues of mutual interest' beyond the framework of the association. With regard to the EEA Council, its responsibilities are essentially political. Hence, it gives 'political impetus in the implementation of' and takes 'political decisions leading to amendments to the [EEA] Agreement'. Most other decisions are left to the EEA Joint Committee, the general guidelines for which the EEA Council lays down.

The association committee is generally regarded as the workhorse of each association, partly because it meets more frequently than the asso-ciation council. In early association agreements, its establishment followed a decision of the association council and was accompanied by the creation of a customs cooperation committee. The more recent EEA and Europe Agreements, however, contain explicit provision for asso-ciation committees to be created. This is because they are viewed as essential to the effective functioning of such wide-ranging associations. Hence, they often deal with the technicalities of the relationship, a point reflected in their composition. Generally, association committees con-sist of representatives of the members of the Council of Ministers, members of the Commission, and representatives of the associate's government, normally at the level of senior civil servant. The more technical nature of association committees is also reflected in the fact that they are often supplemented by association sub-committees as established by the association council.

The third institution common to all associations is the association parliamentary committee (APC), sometimes referred to as the joint parliamentary committee (JPC). Once again, early association agreements made no specific reference to their establishment, but contacts between the European Parliament and the national parliament of individual associates were encouraged and indeed established.[21] The role of APCs is limited. Their purpose, according to the Europe Agreements, is to act as little more than a forum where MPs from the associate's national parliament can meet and exchange views with Members of the European Parliament (MEPs). The APCs can, however, request information regarding the association from, and make recommendations to, the association council. They are also informed of decisions taken by the association council.

In addition to the three common institutions and the association sub-committees already mentioned, other bodies have been created within the context of different associations (see Table 2.4). The first of these is the EC–Turkey Customs Union Joint Committee. This was created in 1996 to monitor the implementation of the recently established customs union between the EC and Turkey. Secondly, there are the trade and economic cooperation committees with Malta and Cyprus. These were established in 1988–89 to 'improve the operation of the institutional mechanisms' of the respective association agreements. A third other body is the EEA Consultative Committee. This brings together members of the EC's Economic and Social Committee and of other bodies representing the social partners in EU and EFTA states. The Committee's role is limited, however, to expressing views on the EEA. No other association agreement with a European state provides for a similar committee, although proposals have recently been made for them to be established in the context of associations with CEE states. Finally, mention should be made of the EFTA Surveillance Authority and the

---

21. In the cases of Greece and Turkey, the reference to contacts appears in the main body of the association agreement. By contrast, and underlining their more minimalist nature, the reference to contacts between the national parliaments of Cyprus and Malta and the European Parliament was relegated to a joint declaration attached to the final act of each agreement.

EFTA Court. These were established in 1994 in line with the requirements of the EEA Agreement. Although not technically institutions of the association, they are integral to the effective functioning of the EEA. The EFTA Surveillance Authority is responsible for monitoring the implementation of the EEA in participating EFTA states and the EFTA Court settles disputes between EFTA states. The existence of these two institutions and the Consultative Committee helps the EEA stand out as the association with the most advanced institutional framework. Confirmation of such prominence can be obtained by examining three other aspects of certain associations. The first of these is the relationship between the association and the EC's decision-making procedures; the second is the existence of political dialogue; and the third is the dispute-settlement procedure.

Table 2.4: Associations and Institutional Frameworks

	Greece	Turkey	Malta	Cyprus	EEA	Europe Agreements
Association						
Council	*	*	*	*	*	*
Committee	(*)	(*)	(*)	(*)	*	*
Subcommittees	(*)	(*)	(*)	(*)	(*)	(*)
Parliamentary Committee	(*)	(*)	(*)	(*)	*	*
Other committees						
Trade and economic cooperation			*	*		
Consultative					*	(*)
Customs union (joint)		*				
Miscellaneous						
EFTA surveillance authority					*	
EFTA court					*	

Note: Parentheses indicate those institutions not specifically mentioned in the association agreement.

With regard to the first of these, there are two examples of associates being offered a privileged access to EC decision-making. Neither, however, entails participation in the actual taking of decisions.[22] Rather, the

22. There is one example of an associate being granted a role in EC decision-making. Greece was scheduled to be involved in decisions concerning unforeseen

views of associates are formally taken into consideration by EC and EU institutions outside the framework of the association council and committee. For example, the upgrading of Turkey's association with the EC to customs union in 1995 was accompanied by the EC committing itself to consult informally Turkish experts when drafting legislation affecting the customs union. Provision was also made for Turkish experts to be involved in the work of selected technical committees that assist the Commission in its work. Such formal access, albeit very limited, clearly suggests that the greater the degree of integration established by the association, the more developed the institutional contacts. The argument is borne out not only by the absence of such access in the early stages of associations but more significantly by arrangements within the EEA. Here, provision exists for a 'continuous information and consultation process' involving the contracting parties prior to the EU Council of Ministers adopting new EC legislation. Termed 'decision-shaping', this process involves the Commission seeking informal advice and formal views on proposed legislation from the EFTA states. While falling well short of the decision-making role so eagerly sought by the EFTA states in the EEA negotiations, the process is novel in that it does place a legal requirement on the Commission to consult experts from non-Member States when developing EC legislative proposals. Moreover, the process accords these experts a similar status to those from EU Member States.[23]

The second discernible difference to be mentioned here concerns those associations that involve political dialogue. Here, attention is drawn to the Europe Agreements, although political dialogue has also been extended to the associations with Cyprus, Malta and Turkey.[24]

---

changes to the CET relating to certain key products: tobacco, dried raisins, rosin, olives, oil of turpentine. At the time it was made clear that by granting such involvement the EEC was not setting a precedent (Oppermann 1962: 504).

23. Articles 99(1) and 100 of the EEA Agreement state respectively that 'the EC Commission shall informally seek advice from experts of the EFTA States *in the same way* as it seeks advice from experts of the EC Member States for the elaboration of its proposals', and 'when drawing up draft measures the EC Commission shall refer to experts of the EFTA States *on the same basis* as it refers to experts of the EC Member States' (emphasis added).

24. In the case of Cyprus, political dialogue initially took place via regular meetings every six months between the Cypriot Foreign Minister and the President of the EC Council of Ministers. Following a decision of the Association Council in

These provide not only for political dialogue to be carried out at ministerial level within the association council, but also for consultations between the respective presidents of the Commission, the Council, and the associated state.[25] Provision is also made in each agreement for meetings to take place at the level of political directors (senior officials) and through diplomatic channels; for the EC to provide regular information on issues dealt with within the framework of European Political Cooperation/CFSP; and for the use of 'any other means' to consolidate, develop and step up the dialogue. Finally, political dialogue at the parliamentary level is to take place in the association parliamentary committees.

The third area for discussion is dispute settlement. In the case of the minimalist associations agreements with Malta and Cyprus, no mechanism is included. In more advanced agreements (Greece, Turkey, Cyprus since 1988, Europe Agreements), the dispute settlement procedure is straightforward. It involves the issue being referred to the association council. If the association council is unable to settle the dispute, three arbitrators are appointed and decide the matter by majority.[26] Both the EC and the associate are then obliged to take the necessary measures to implement the arbitrators' decision. A different procedure is provided for in the EEA Agreement. Here, the need to resolve disputes is accompanied by the need to ensure the homogeneity of the EEA. Hence, where the EEA Joint Committee is unable to settle the dispute and the matter concerns a provision of the EEA identical to one in the Treaty of Rome, the dispute may be referred to the European Court of Justice (ECJ) for a ruling. In cases where the EEA Joint Committee does not refer the matter to the ECJ, either the relevant part

December 1992, meetings involving the Cypriot President have also been held as part of European Council summits.

25. The references to the respective presidents appear in the Europe Agreements with Bulgaria, the Czech Republic, Poland and Slovakia. The Hungarian and Romanian agreements are less specific, referring to consultations taking place at the 'highest political level'. Later Europe Agreements refer to political dialogue taking place 'within the multilateral framework and according to the forms and practices established with the associated countries of central Europe'. The multilateral framework for political dialogue was established in 1993 (see p. 87).

26. In the association agreements with Greece and Turkey provision is made for disputes to be submitted to the ECJ 'or to any other existing court or tribunal' before being sent to arbitration.

of the EEA Agreement may be suspended or safeguard measures may be taken. Other matters are referred to arbitration as above.

Although the EEA does not contain explicit provision for political dialogue, its institutional framework does stand out as an example of how associations can involve a close institutional as well as legal relationship between the EC and associates. This is not surprising given the scope of the EEA. If participating EFTA states are obliged to adopt the existing and future *acquis* relating to the internal market and its flanking policies, then the EEA has to involve an advanced form of institutional relationship. Yet even where the obligations placed on the associate are extensive, the EC's desire to retain decision-making autonomy rules out participation in its decision-making procedures. Even in its most developed forms to date, association involves at best only decision-shaping. As the discussion in subsequent chapters shows, this considerably undermines the attraction of association.

Table 2.5: Associations, Decision-Making and Dispute Settlement

	Greece	Turkey	Malta	Cyprus	EEA	Europe Agreements
Decision shaping		(*)			*	
Political dialogue		(*)	(*)	(*)		*
Dispute settlement						
ECJ ruling	*	*			*	
Arbitration	*	*		*	*	*
None			*	*		

Note: Parentheses indicate that there is no specific mention in the original association agreement.

The Question of Membership

The discussion so far has concentrated on the purpose, content and structure of associations as if they were a form of permanent relationship between the EC and one or more non-Member States. This can be done since all associations are designed to create durable, long-term ties. Yet it is impossible to examine the different forms of association without considering their relationship to the question of membership of the EC/EU. As indicated in the introduction, almost all European states which have entered into associations have at some point submitted a membership application. The only two states not to have done so are Iceland and Liechtenstein. Is it therefore the intention of the parties that sign the association agreement that the associate eventually becomes a member of the EU? If so, is the association specifically designed to facilitate such an objective?

Ostensibly, when examining the association agreements concluded with Greece and Turkey the answer to these two questions is 'yes'. The preamble to both agreements states that:

> the support given by the European Economic Community to the efforts of the [Greek/Turkish] people to improve their standard of living will facilitate the Accession of [Greece/Turkey] to the Community at a later date.

Reference to membership is also contained in the actual text of each agreement. Article 72 of the Athens Agreement and Article 28 of the Ankara Agreement state:

> As soon as the operation of this Agreement has advanced far enough to justify envisaging full acceptance by [Greece/Turkey] of the obligations arising out of the Treaty establishing the European Economic Community, the Contracting Parties shall examine the possibility of the Accession of [Greece/Turkey] to the Community.

Such statements provide a clear indication of the purpose of each association. Although economically Greece and Turkey were not sufficiently developed to be members of the EEC in the early 1960s, membership was the strategic objective of the association. Having the two states as members would have its advantages. Not only would it integrate Greece and Turkey further into Euro-Atlantic structures thereby strengthening NATO's south-eastern flank, it would also help promote regional stability and more stable relations between the two states. The relevant statements in the Athens and Ankara agreements certainly implied a strong commitment on the part of the EEC to eventual Greek and Turkish membership.

Indeed, the key references noted have been interpreted as a promise of membership. The wording is, however, open to more restrictive interpretations. These emphasize the absence of any legal requirement on the part of the EC to admit either of the two associates. Technically, the agreements are designed simply to *facilitate* accession. Moreover, the contracting parties are only obliged to examine the *possibility* of accession; no actual obligation to admit the associate exists. Commission circles certainly support such a view, regarding the agreements with Greece and Turkey as 'potential-membership association agree-

ment[s]'.[27] Whatever interpretation is accepted, there is no denying that
the references to accession in the preamble and the respective articles
are the most explicit to be found in any association agreements. Hence,
particularly given the fact that Greece joined the EC in 1981, membership is regarded as the feature that distinguishes the agreements. Labels
attached to them by academic commentators underline this. Flaesch-
Mougin, for example, refers to them as 'pre-accession associations'
(1980: 248).[28] Indeed, the association agreements with Greece and
Turkey are unique in referring to accession as an explicit strategic
objective of all the contracting parties. Later agreements would not go
so far.

This can clearly be seen with regard to Malta and Cyprus. The
agreements that the two states signed with the EC in the early 1970s do
not contain a single reference to membership. This was despite the fact
that the Maltese at least were keen on acceding to the EC at some point
in the future. Indeed, the proposals for association put forward by
Malta's Nationalist government suggested that the second stage of the
association could lead to membership. Moreover, on signing the association agreement in 1970, the Maltese government indicated that it
would submit an application for membership at a future, yet unspecified, date.

The decision not to include a reference to membership lay with the
EC. The associations with Greece and Turkey were not developing as
envisaged and there was no desire on the part of the EC to commit itself
and predetermine future relations. This was made clear to the Maltese
and for good reason. The domestic political situation on the island did
not bode well for the association. With the EC-hostile Labour Party
likely to win the 1971 general election, it would have been inopportune
to embark on an accession-oriented association. Moreover, the EC had
no desire to set any precedents at a time when consideration was being
given to the development of a global Mediterranean policy and it was
about to negotiate association agreements with various other Mediterranean states. Such a reason partly explains the absence of any reference to membership in Cyprus's agreement signed in 1972. Yet here,
there is also the fact that membership did not feature prominently on

27. See Edmund Wellenstein (1979: 416) who was formerly the Commission's
Director-General for External Relations.
28. The French original is *associations préadhésion*. See also Becker (1983:
1300) who uses the label 'accession associations' *(Beitrittsassoziationen)*.

the government's agenda for relations with the EC.

Despite the lack of any reference in either the Maltese or Cypriot agreement to the association having membership as a strategic objective, both agreements were regarded in some quarters as leading to accession. Commissioner Dahrendorf certainly seemed to believe that Malta would one day join the EC.[29] Commentators would also subsequently argue that membership was envisaged as the ultimate goal of the two associations (Luchaire 1975: 431). That said, neither agreement was obliging the EC formally to consider either Malta or Cyprus for admission at a later date. Therefore, although membership was not being ruled out, neither was association officially seen as a stepping-stone to membership. The situation would later change (see pp. 104-106). But, in terms of how association was evolving as a mechanism for external relations with European non-Member States, clearly the early enthusiasm for a link with membership was waning.[30] This would be confirmed in the 1980s when the EC once again began using association in a European context. Indeed, when devising and negotiating the Europe Agreements, considerable effort was made to promote them as establishing sui generis associations. Before the Europe Agreements were devised, however, efforts were under way to establish the EEA. With this proposed association potentially involving seven non-Member States, views regarding its relationship to the question of membership differed.

As far as the EC was concerned, the EEA was originally conceived as a medium-term, if not permanent, alternative to membership. The fact that the idea of an EEA agreement was first proposed by the Commission President, Jacques Delors in January 1989, is significant. At a time when the EC was becoming more dynamic and the Commission was keen to further integration, there was no desire to be distracted by the admission of any new members. Hence, in April 1988, the Commission declared that priority should be given to deepening over widening. It announced that the EC would not be enlarging until after the scheduled completion of the internal market on 31 December 1992. The EEA could therefore serve as a waiting room for EFTA states keen

29. See his comments to the European Parliament on 9 February 1971 in *JOCE Annexe*, No. 133, February 1971, p. 26.

30. This does not mean to say no consideration was being given to using association as a stepping-stone to membership. Khol (1985), for example, advocated that Austria establish an association with the EC as a precursor to accession.

on membership. Indeed, given that the Austrian government at this time
was preparing a membership application (which it submitted in July
1989), there was a clear need for the EC to offer a medium-term alternative. Hence, Pedersen argues that the proposal to establish the EEA
was specifically designed as 'a tactical ploy, meant to cool down
Austrian bilateralism in an attempt to gain time' (1990: 73).[31] There
was little desire within the Commission to see plans for greater political
integration (e.g. towards a common foreign and security policy) among
the EC's Member States threatened by the admission of neutral countries. Hence, concluding an agreement that would involve EFTA states
in the internal market and its flanking policies could deter those EFTA
states that were neutral from seeking membership.

For most EFTA states, Delors' proposal for an EEA agreement was
greeted warmly since it provided most of them with what appeared to
be a potential alternative to membership.[32] The initial enthusiasm for
the EEA soon began to wane, however. First, it became increasingly
clear during negotiations that there were limits to what the EC was
willing to include in any agreement. A major concern was that the
EFTA states would be offered only a limited decision-shaping rather
than decision-making role regarding future EC legislation affecting the
EEA. Secondly, with the end of the Cold War and the collapse of the
USSR, the main barrier for some EFTA states to applying for EC
membership—neutrality—appeared to be losing its relevance. Hence,
many governments began to consider openly whether the ideal type of
relations with the EC should be membership rather than simply partici-

31. The Austrian government, however, never regarded the EEA as a serious
alternative to membership.

32. This was particularly true of Norway. Indeed, there is strong argument
which says that the inspiration behind Delors' proposal for the EEA Agreement
came from the Norwegian Prime Minister, Gro Harlem Brundtland. During a
meeting in late 1988, Brundtland is alleged to have urged Delors to propose a new
EC–EFTA partnership so as to help prevent a 'premature' membership debate in
Norway. Brundtland's fear was that any debate would reopen, both within the
ruling Labour Party and the country as a whole, the wounds created by the 1972
referendum on EC membership. In the light of Delors' own concerns regarding
widening and deepening, he was naturally sympathetic to his fellow socialist's
position. The arguments in support of this 'Brundtland factor' are strengthened by
the fact that it was the Norwegian Prime Minister who called a meeting of EFTA
heads of government for March 1989. This was the first such meeting for almost
five years and clearly timetabled so that it could respond to any EC initiative.

pation in the EEA. To the surprise of few, the Swedish government was the first to signal a shift in policy. In July 1991, it followed the Austrian example and submitted an application for EC membership. This helped trigger an application from Finland before the EEA agreement was even signed. Applications soon followed from Switzerland and Norway (see Appendix 2). Moreover, the Lisbon European Council in June 1992 announced that the next enlargement negotiations would be with EFTA states intent on membership. For EFTA states, with the exception of Iceland and Liechtenstein, the EEA became little more than a stepping-stone to membership.

Such developments clearly did not go unnoticed in the negotiations towards the EEA, although the only reference to membership contained in the agreement is brief and non-committal. The fourteenth recital of the preamble simply states that 'this Agreement shall not prejudice in any way the possibility of any EFTA state to accede to the European Communities'. Hence, from a legal point of view, the EEA agreement, and by implication association, has no direct link with membership. This is despite the fact that, as noted above, the EEA involves a relationship that falls only narrowly short of membership.

The fact that participation in the EEA is neither designed to lead to nor contains any promise of EU membership means that it cannot easily be viewed as a stepping-stone to membership. It is more appropriate to treat this advanced form of association as a type of waiting room where a state intent on acceding to the EU can prepare itself for possible future entry and await the call from the EU to negotiate entry. This is indeed how the EEA came to be viewed by the majority of EFTA states. Participants accepted that no state would be admitted into the EC/EU until the latter decided to enlarge. In the meantime, a state's best strategy was to assume many of the obligations of membership in anticipation of an invitation from the EU to negotiate accession. Simply being part of the EEA does not, however, guarantee an invitation. This is intentional since there are EFTA states that have always viewed the EEA, as the EC intended, as an alternative to membership. Indeed, when the EEA was conceived every effort was being made to avoid any link between association and membership.

This was even more apparent with regard to the development in 1990–91 of the Europe Agreements with CEE states. Here, there was considerable pressure on the EC to establish a direct link between association and membership as CEE states expressed their desire ultimately to accede to the EC. The pressure was strongly resisted though. Indeed, when the Commission published its initial proposal for what would become Europe Agreements in early 1990, great emphasis was placed on the sui generis nature of the associations to be created. The communication stated clearly that the agreements would be 'of special value in themselves'. Hence, they would not contain any commitment concerning membership (EC Commission 1990b). Rather, the agreements would help the CEE countries overcome the problems of the economic and political reform process. Hasty promises to the CEE countries about membership had to be avoided. There was no desire to commit the EC to eastern enlargement when there was no guarantee that the transition processes on which the countries were embarking would be successful. Also there were ongoing concerns about the desirability of enlargement when the majority view within the EC was that priority should be given to deepening integration. It was better to establish associations to address more immediate needs rather than focus on the somewhat distant prospect of membership.

For the CEE countries, however, accession to the EC was a key foreign policy goal. There was, therefore, a clear preference to see the EC commit itself to eastern enlargement at a future date and establish the Europe Agreements as stepping-stones to membership (Lippert 1990: 123). Membership would not only ensure access to EC markets and funds, it would also help ensure the irreversibility of economic and political reform and provide some implicit security guarantees to the CEE states. However, all that the EC was willing to do initially was to reassure the CEE countries that association would not affect the possibility of them gaining membership. Membership would not be an objective of the Europe Agreements (EC Commission 1990a).

In the course of negotiations with Czechoslovakia, Hungary and Poland, however, the EC did eventually relent and a compromise was reached. A first concession was the inclusion of a statement recognizing each state's membership aspirations. Later, it was also accepted that the proposed statement would include reference to the association contributing to the attainment of membership. Hence, when the agreements were signed, the final recital of each preamble stated:

> Recognizing the fact that the [associate's] ultimate objective is to become a member of the Community, and that this Association, in the view of the parties, will help the [associate] to achieve this objective.[33]

33. The actual wording used does differ in some agreements. In the agreement

From a legal perspective, the implications of the provisions are clear (Müller-Graff 1997: 34). First, the EC and its Member States are aware of the associate's intention to seek membership; secondly, the EC and its Member States have no contractual obligation regarding the granting of membership to the associate; and thirdly, the EC, its Member States and the associate regard the agreement as assisting the achievement of the objective of the associate. Consequently, the first Europe Agreements, at least when they were signed, were not viewed as stepping-stones to membership. In fact, the EC regarded the recital as a major concession even if it did lack the clarity and sense of shared purpose of

Table 2.6: Associations and the Question of Membership

	Greece/ Turkey	Cyprus/ Malta	EEA	Europe Agreements
No reference to membership		*		
EEC support to facilitate accession at a later date	*			
Possibility of accession to be examined	*			
Agreement not to prejudge possibility of accession			*	
Membership recognized as objective of associate				*
Association to help associate achieve membership				*

the provisions contained in the association agreements with Greece and Turkey. Within a few years, however, views changed. As the next chapter shows, by the time Estonia, Latvia, Lithuania and Slovenia signed their Europe Agreements, attitudes towards the associations being established with the CEE states had moved on. A direct link between association and membership was being established.[34]

with Hungary, the phrase 'Having in mind' as opposed to 'Recognizing' is used. In the agreements with the Czech Republic and Slovakia, the preambles state that the ultimate objective is 'to accede to the Community'. In the agreements with Estonia, Latvia and Lithuania, reference is to membership of the European Union. Also, rather than 'this Association', reference is made to 'association through this Agreement'.

34. Hence, the preambles to the Europe Agreements with Estonia, Latvia, Lithuania and Slovenia acknowledge the 'accession preparation strategy' adopted by the Essen European Council in December 1994 (see p. 107).

Summary

The flexibility of association can lead to various forms of relationship being established. Aims and rationales differ as do strategic objectives. Likewise, different associations have different trade regimes. The scope of envisaged cooperation is rarely the same in any two agreements. There are clear differences between associations in terms of commitments which the agreements entail. Added to this, the relationship between association and membership differs from one type of relationship to another. This does not mean there are no similarities between associations. All share the basic aim of trade promotion. The notion that the relationship can and should evolve is at least implicit in each agreement. Also, all associations have the same basic institutional framework and all associates remain outside the EC/EU. Association should not be viewed, therefore, as some form of semi- or quasi-membership. Association and membership can, though, be talked about in the same sentence.

No association has been established without some consideration being given to its relationship to membership. For the most part, the EC/EU has sought to deny any link. Hence, association can be seen very much as an alternative to membership. Yet for those associates intent on membership the link is there. Even if it is rarely explicit, the desire to see association as leading to or facilitating membership has always been made known. As the discussion in the next chapter shows, such a desire has generally intensified with experiences of association. In most cases, the EC/EU has gradually acquiesced to demands that the link be made explicit. Hence, except where the associate wishes to remain outside the EC/EU, associations have eventually been perceived as stepping-stones to membership.

Yet, as will be seen, experiences of association suggest that the relationship is not necessarily the stepping-stone to membership that most would wish it to be. Few states have enjoyed their association and there are few examples so far where the relationship has functioned well and actually led to the associate acceding to the EC/EU. In several instances, it is very much despite rather than because of association that a state seeks and obtains membership. In other cases, states apply for membership because of the shortcomings of association. Despite its flexibility and the various forms that association can take, experiences of association and the lessons that can be drawn from them show that it is rarely regarded as a long-term alternative to EC/EU membership.

3 |

Experiences of Association

The discussion so far has been based on the content and aims of the association agreement. While they help us to understand what associations are intended to involve, they say little about the reality of association. The purpose of this chapter is to explore the actual experiences of association. This is done by examining how well the institutional framework has functioned; the impact of association on the development of trade relations; the extent of cooperation pursued; the financial assistance made available; the way in which the purpose of association has shifted in terms of its link to membership; and the contribution that association has played in preparing associates for accession to the EC/EU. The first two sections deal, however, with the establishment of the associations and the difficulties that have existed in maintaining some of them as functioning relations.

What emerges from the various discussions is that associates and the EC have had mixed experiences of association. Rarely have the early associations functioned properly and satisfactorily. Associates have not always obtained the anticipated benefits from the relationship whether it is in terms of trade or aid. Also, cooperation has generally been limited. All the same, most associations have been enhanced and upgraded. More significantly, most have seen their strategic objective altered following a membership application. Today, the majority of associations are treated as if they were stepping-stones to membership. Whether they can accurately be described as such is open to question. To date, associations have made only a limited contribution to the achievement of membership.

Establishing the Associations: Ratification

On each occasion when an association agreement has been signed, great emphasis has been placed on how the association represents a new era in the development of relations between the EC and the state or states concerned. The signing ceremony provides opportunities all round for self-congratulation. For the EC, the conclusion of an agreement helps to sustain the desired image of an open Community willing and committed to involve non-Member States in its integration efforts. For the non-Member States, the occasion is used to signal further progress in the pursuit of integration with the EC and, in most cases, an irreversible step on the way to membership.

In many cases, however, the enthusiasm for association that is so evident on such occasions soon evaporates. For non-Member States, this is often accompanied by frustration and a degree of disillusionment. This is not because of any sudden discovery that the signed agreement contains major lacunae, but because ratification within the EC is rarely, if ever, accorded top priority. Hence, it tends to be a long drawn out process which can last not months, but years. Indeed, whereas associates-to-be tend to complete ratification within six months, the EC takes on average well over a year. In some instances, ratification has taken over two-and-a-half years (see Table 3.1). The essential reason for this delay is the fact that all association agreements signed with European non-Member States, with the exception of those signed with Malta and Cyprus, have been mixed agreements. Therefore, not only do they require (since 1987) the assent of the European Parliament, they must also be ratified by each of the Member States before they can enter into force. For its part, the European Parliament has usually acted swiftly. Since it was first required to give its assent to association agreements, it has never taken more than ten months to ratify an agreement. This even applies to the 1995 EC–Turkey customs union agreement which the European Parliament threatened to reject because of concerns over Turkey's human rights record. By contrast, the Member States have often been exceptionally slow in obtaining domestic parliamentary approval. The first set of Europe Agreements, for example, took more than two years to be ratified. Signed in December 1991, the agreements with Hungary and Poland did not enter into force until 1 February 1994. Initially, ratification was scheduled for completion by November 1992. Later Europe Agreements with the Baltic States and Slovenia took even longer—more than two-and-a-half years. Some compensation was at hand. As noted below (p. 75), the trade provisions of each Europe Agreement entered into force separately either following the conclusion of so-called 'interim'

Table 3.1: Ratification of Association Agreements

	Signed	Ratification by associate	Ratification by EP	Entry into force	Ratification (in months)[a]
Greece	09.07.1961	28.02.1962	n.a.	01.11.1962	16
Turkey	12.09.1963	15.01.1964	n.a.	01.12.1964	15.5
Malta	05.12.1970	n.k.	n.a.	01.04.1971	4
Cyprus	19.12.1972	n.k.	n.a.	01.06.1973	5.5
EEA Agreement	02.05.1992	—	28.10.1992	01.01.1994	20
EEA Protocol	17.03.1993	—	23.05.1993	01.01.1994	9.5
Hungary	16.12.1991	17.11.1992	15.09.1992	01.02.1994	25.5
Poland	16.12.1991	04.07.1992	15.09.1992	01.02.1994	25.5
Czechoslovakia	16.12.1991	22.04.1992[b]	—	—	—
Romania	01.02.1993	n.k.	27.10.1993	01.02.1995	24
Bulgaria	08.03.1993	15.04.1993	27.10.1993	01.02.1995	23
Czech Republic	04.10.1993	n.k.	27.10.1993	01.02.1995	16
Slovakia	04.10.1993	17.12.1993	27.10.1993	01.02.1995	16
Estonia	12.06.1995	01.08.1995	15.11.1995	01.02.1998	31.5
Latvia	12.06.1995	31.08.1995	15.11.1995	01.02.1998	31.5
Lithuania	12.06.1995	05.08.1996	15.11.1995	01.02.1998	31.5
Slovenia	10.06.1996	15.07.1997	24.10.1996	01.02.1999	32

[a] The figures are approximate and represent the number of months between the signing and entry into force of an agreement. Technically, ratification is shorter since the entry into force of an agreement normally takes place on the first day of the second month after the final instrument of ratification has been deposited.
[b] Parliamentary ratification. Final ratification by the President did not take place owing to the decision to split the country following the election results of June 1992.

agreements or through the existence of previously signed free trade agreements.

Delays in ratification have never been the consequence of serious opposition to an agreement. Strains in bilateral relations have, however, affected the speed of ratification. A case in point is Italy's protracted consideration of Slovenia's Europe Agreement in 1996–98. Only after the Slovenian government agreed to compensate ethnic Italians who fled their properties on the Istrian peninsula at the end of World War II did the Italian government set in motion the ratification process. Also, concerns about the impact of a proposed agreement on a Member State's foreign trade have led to delays. The Italian government indicated in 1961 that ratification of Greece's association agreement could not be guaranteed. Yet the main reasons for delay have more to do with either technicalities or agendas of the parliaments in the Member States than with the association agreement per se. On the former, excuses advanced for slow ratification of the Europe Agreements have included the unavailability of texts, translation problems and legal difficulties. As for the latter, delays in ratifying the EEA Agreement reflected pre-occupation with ratification of the Maastricht Treaty. In the UK, for example, Tory Eurosceptics threatened to jeopardize the passage of the EEA as part of their tactics for blocking ratification of the Maastricht Treaty. In turn, the Spanish government threatened to hold up ratification in protest over the UK's slow progress with ratifying the Maastricht Treaty.

The immediate impact of slow ratification is a sense of sheer frustration on the part of the associate-to-be. This was certainly evident with the first Europe Agreements. On numerous occasions, Polish and Hungarian leaders and officials openly voiced their concerns about the delays in ratification. The agreements had been signed in good faith with the purpose of facilitating the countries' 'return to Europe'. Failure to ratify swiftly on the part of the EC suggested only a limited commitment to this goal. A second consequence of slow ratification is the impact it has on the establishment of the association. Technically, the association is not established until the association agreement has entered into force. Hence, neither can the envisaged institutional framework be set up, nor can political dialogue be pursued. Equally, binding decisions concerning the development of the association cannot formally be adopted and opportunities for closer cooperation may be limited. Admittedly, in most cases, use can be made of existing institutions. Most associates can rely on dialogue and cooperation via joint committees set up under earlier trade agreements. In the case of Greece, a so-called 'interim committee' was used. In the case of the CEE countries, fora for multilateral political dialogue were set up as early as 1992. All the same, the existence and effective functioning of the association institutions carries symbolic importance, especially for the associate. They signify involvement and integration. Delaying their establishment can mean that opportunities to promote a dynamic relationship are missed. Thirdly, delays in ratification have also affected the associate-to-be's access to any trade concessions granted by the EC. This was certainly true of the early association agreements with Greece and Turkey. The matter has, however, rarely occurred with more recent agreements. When signing Europe Agreements, the EC has also signed so-called 'interim agreements'. These have contained trade-related provisions identical to those in the Europe Agreements and have been concluded under Article 113 (133) of the Treaty of Rome.[1] This has meant that they could enter into force within a matter of a few months.[2]

Maintaining the Associations

Once established, most associations function effectively. This is certainly true of the EEA and the associations created by the Europe Agreements. So far, they have functioned on a continuous basis. They are still relatively young though, and if the experiences of early associations are to be repeated, then there is no guarantee that they will

1. The interim agreements appear in the following issues of the *OJ*: Poland, *OJ* L114 (30 April 1992); Czechoslovakia, *OJ* L115 (30 April 1992); Hungary, *OJ* L116 (30 April 1992); Romania, *OJ* L81 (2 April 1993); Bulgaria, *OJ* L323 (23 December 1993); Slovenia, *OJ* L344 (31 October 1996). In the case of the three Baltic states, free trade agreements had been concluded prior to the Europe Agreements being signed: Estonia, *OJ* L373 (31 December 1994); Latvia, *OJ* L374 (31 December 1994); Lithuania, *OJ* L375 (31 December 1994). Consequently, there was no need for interim agreements.

2. The entry into force of Bulgaria's interim agreement was delayed, however, when it became hostage to differences within the EC over safeguard clauses and the trade concessions being granted to CEE countries. Although signed on the same day as the Europe Agreement (8 March 1993), the interim agreement did not enter into force until 31 December 1993. The delay led the Bulgarian government to seek compensation for the alleged costs (US$ 200 million) of late entry into force (*Agence Europe*, 11 November 1993: 8).

remain fully operational. Each of the associations with Greece, Turkey and Malta, albeit for differing reasons, effectively became a non-relationship at some point. The development of relations with Greece and Turkey was halted by domestic political upheaval in the two countries, and in the case of Malta governments in the period 1971–86 showed limited interest in the EC. Consequently, experiences of association have tended to be limited. Moreover, in the case of Cyprus, its association failed to develop as anticipated. The EC, eager to see the de facto division of the island after 1974 overcome, was reluctant to agree to an upgrading of the association to a customs union since there was no guarantee that this would benefit all communities in Cyprus.

Of the four associations that have experienced difficulties, the first to suffer was that between the EC and Greece. Following the Colonels' coup in 1967 and the overthrow of democracy, the EC decided that the association should be reduced to *gestion courante* (current administration). This meant that all aspects of the association agreement, with the exception of those carrying specific obligations relating to tariff reductions, were effectively 'frozen' until democracy was restored in 1974 (Coufoudakis 1977). While this allowed for trade relations to be maintained, it did mean that no cooperation could take place and financial assistance was suspended. So, for seven years, the association essentially became a non-relationship. Even subsequently, there was little enthusiasm for the association. In part, this reflected the fact that the relationship had not functioned particularly satisfactorily prior to 1967. As early as 1964, Greek officials were heard criticizing the association: exports had not increased as anticipated, financial assistance had not been as great as forecast, and little progress had been made with the harmonization of agricultural policies. Soon Commission officials too were acknowledging that results had not been entirely satisfactory and that there were 'points of friction' in relations. Progress with common action was limited and the EC was being accused of not paying due attention to Greek interests (Saclé 1968: 12). That said, nobody wished for the relationship to be abandoned. After 1974 though, the new Greek government focused its attention squarely on EC membership. Following its application for membership on 12 June 1975 and the opening of accession negotiations just over a year later, little use was made of the association.

For Greece, accession to the EC in 1981 compensated for any dissatisfaction with the association. Turkey, however, has not received any

3. *Experiences of Association*   77

such compensation. Despite submitting a membership application in 1987, it remains firmly outside the EU. Moreover, Turkey finds itself in an association which has rarely proved to be a satisfactory relationship for either itself or the EC. At various points since it was established in 1964, the association has either received scant attention or appeared to be on the verge of total breakdown. The blame for this can be placed at the doors of both the EC and Turkey. During the early years of the association, the EC appeared to pursue a policy of 'benign neglect' (Kramer 1988: 41,) while Turkey's approach amounted to little more than laissez-faire (Ilkin 1990: 38-39). As for the 1970s, various issues made relations tense and problematic. These included domestic political upheaval in Turkey, the Turkish invasion of northern Cyprus in 1974, accusations of EC protectionism, and the EC's favourable response to Greece's membership application. Not surprisingly, relations at this time have been described as being characterized by 'disenchantment' and 'malaise' (Penrose 1981: 63-69). The association would, however, remain in place. Yet before any progress could be made, the association experienced a five-year 'freeze' following the military takeover in Turkey on September 1980.

Once democracy was restored in Turkey in 1983–84 the opportunity existed to revitalize the association. EC preoccupation with its own internal agenda and Iberian enlargement and concerns over the human rights situation in Turkey meant progress was slow. The situation was compounded by the presence of Greece as a member of the EC. Grievances over Cyprus meant that it was threatening to veto all developments in the association. Indeed, relations endured a further period of deterioration in the period 1985–88. A particular low point came in 1988 when the Turkish Foreign Minister walked out of a meeting of the Association Council following disagreements over the Cyprus question. No subsequent meetings at ministerial level were held until 30 September 1991. At the time, the future of the association seemed bleak, particularly since Turkey had by now applied for EC membership. The application was submitted on 14 April 1987.

The EC's response to the application was to reject Turkish membership in the short and medium term (EC Commission 1989). Instead, the EC was keen to revitalize the association through completion of the customs union, intensified cooperation, and strengthened political and cultural links. Such proposals were supported by Turkey and agreement was eventually reached in November 1992 to resume work towards

completing the customs union and creating political dialogue between
Turkey and the EC. Negotiations, often strained, eventually led to
agreement on a customs union accord and progress towards the release
of financial aid. Key to the agreement was a deal providing Greece with
a timetable for Cypriot membership of the EU. The Greek veto on
developments in EU–Turkey relations was temporarily lifted. The
customs union agreement was duly signed on 22 December 1995.
Seemingly, the association was alive again. The existence of a pro-
Islamic government in Turkey during 1996–97 coupled with Turkish de
facto exclusion from the EU's plans for enlargement did, however, lead
to a new crisis in relations. While the association did not appear to be
under immediate threat, the crisis re-emphasized the turbulence surrounding EU–Turkish relations and the difficulties that have existed in
maintaining what has become the EC's longest standing association.

Turning to Malta, here too the history of the association has not been
problem-free. This is not to say that the relationship has been bedev-
illed with disagreements between the EC and Malta. Rather, owing to
the position of the Maltese government in 1971–86 the association in
effect was a non-relationship. On gaining power in 1971, the Maltese
Labour Party under Dom Mintoff demanded a renegotiation of the
association agreement and additional trade concessions. Neither was
forthcoming. As a consequence, the government adopted a rather
ambiguous approach to the EC. On the one hand, it tolerated, rather
than implemented, the association. At times, it even appeared willing to
see the association agreement lapse. On the other hand, the government
was willing to seek trade concessions from the EC, but its abrasive
approach and use of threats and aggression did not win any friends in
Brussels. Not surprisingly, the association failed to evolve into a
meaningful mechanism for promoting integration and cooperation.

Despite the ambivalent, if not aggressive, approach of the Labour
government to relations with the EC, the first stage of the association
was implemented. However, the move to stage two, due to start on
1 April 1976, was never negotiated. The Labour government was
opposed to a customs union and in 1981 stated that it had no desire to
see the association proceed to the second stage. Instead, the first stage
was simply extended. Initially authorized via bilateral decisions, the EC
ended up adopting these unilaterally from 1980 until 1988. All the
same, supplementary and additional protocols were signed to take
account of the EC's 1973 enlargement and provided Malta with

improved access to the EC market. Moreover, an Additional Protocol in 1976 ensured that Maltese industrial goods could enter the EC tariff-free. However, the association only really existed in name. As long as Mintoff remained in office, both the full implementation and further development of the association were effectively ruled out. For Mintoff, there was no real desire to improve relations, other than to exact further trade concessions and financial aid from an EC viewed essentially as a milch cow (Rossi 1986: 320). Equally, for the EC, there was no compelling reason to respond to the demands of its 'greedy and politically confused' associate thereby setting a precedent for other Mediterranean non-Member States (Redmond 1993: 109-110).

Such a state of affairs did not really change until after the Nationalist Party came to power in 1987, although the Labour government under Karmed Mifsud Bonnici (1984–87) did adopt a friendlier attitude towards the EC. Hence, talks were held on the possible development of a 'special relationship', and at the institutional level, the Association Council resumed its activities on 13 May 1986. Representatives from the European Parliament and of the Maltese House of Representatives also held their first reciprocal visits in June and September 1986. And, once in power, the Nationalist Party embarked on a policy of pursuing closer relations with the EC. The Association Council began to meet more frequently and a supplementary protocol aimed at improving trade relations and the functioning of the association was signed.[3] Regular dialogue meetings were also to be held between Malta and the EC within the context of European Political Cooperation from 1988 onwards. Parliamentary contacts were also becoming more frequent. And, in 1988, the European Parliament adopted the Prag report recommending the creation of 'a new and closer Association' between the EC and Malta. The association at last appeared to be functioning. All the same, as seen below (p. 105), the decision of the Maltese government to apply for membership in July 1990 meant that there was only limited enthusiasm for the relationship except as a stepping-stone to membership. Yet when the Labour Party was in government for a brief period in 1996–98, it expressed a willingness for the association agreement to be upgraded to include cooperation in a range of areas. The return to power of the Nationalist Party in September 1998 saw, however, a reactivation of the membership bid. Once again, association was not being viewed as the ideal basis for relations.

3.   *OJ* L81, 23 March 1989.

In contrast to Maltese attitudes, Cypriot governments have generally been keen to build up the association, particularly during the 1970s and 1980s. At the time, however, the EC was reluctant to see the relationship develop. This was essentially a reaction to the dual invasion of Cyprus in 1974, first by Greek officers and shortly afterwards by the Turkish army. Indeed, owing to the de facto division of the island and the fact that there was no guarantee that the association could therefore benefit the entire island, the EC refused to respond to requests from the Cypriot government for the relationship to move to the second stage as envisaged. For the EC, democracy and territorial integrity were deemed to be indispensable conditions for the normal functioning of the association. Such a position was maintained until 1977. Once the prospects for a diplomatic settlement to the island's division improved, the EC did indicate a willingness to strengthen the association. Although welcome, the Additional Protocol which was duly signed failed to move the association beyond the first stage.[4] This was despite a concerted effort on the part of the Cypriot government to see a customs union established. The EC remained reluctant to support such a development, conscious of the limited progress being made in the intercommunal talks between the Greek and Turkish Cypriots, and concerned that the association should benefit the entire island. Once Greece joined the EC in 1981, its support for the Cypriot cause increased the likelihood of a move to the second stage. Nevertheless, growing divisions within the EC over improved market access for Cypriot agricultural products, a prioritization to reform of the Common Agricultural Policy (CAP), enlargement and a new Mediterranean policy prevented any progress. The EC's own domestic policy agenda therefore displaced the political situation in Cyprus as the main obstacle to the intensification of relations after 1980 (Tsardanidis 1988: 366-68).

Internal differences over trade relations with Cyprus persisted through the first half of the 1980s mainly due to Italy and France linking new concessions to a satisfactory reform of the CAP. Indeed, the apparent deadlock in the development of relations led to concerns that the association could erupt into crisis (Tsardanidis 1988: 346). Such pessimism was unjustified. Negotiations on the move to the second stage of the association began in December 1985 with a new protocol providing for a two-phased transition to the second stage being signed

4. *OJ* L339, 28 December 1977.

on 19 October 1987. It duly entered into force on 1 January 1988.[5] Cyprus's association was now back on course. With the launch of institutionalized political dialogue in November 1988 and the signing of a third financial protocol worth ECU 62 million 12 months later, the association was seemingly becoming a worthwhile relationship. The effective functioning of the association in the 1990s and the steady progress being made towards customs union by 2002 presented a convincing case.

The Functioning of Institutions

Even where there have been difficulties in maintaining associations, each has seen the establishment of an institutional framework to manage the relationship. In each association to date, at least three core institutions have been created: the association council, the association committee, and the association parliamentary committee. Association Councils have in turn set up various customs cooperation committees and association sub-committees (see Table 3.2). In the case of the EEA, the Consultative Committee has also been established. Similar committees have also been proposed for CEE associations. If such bilateral institutions were not enough, most current associates also enjoy participation in a multilateral framework of institutionalized links with the EC/EU (see below). Understandably therefore, links between the EC and associated states have been strengthened. Ministers and officials from the associated states have become more familiar with EC/EU processes, and EC/EU officials have become more aware of the priorities, concerns and needs of the associated states. Yet the existence of association institutions, as with the establishment of associations per se, does not guarantee a harmonious and balanced relationship being developed between associates and the EC. As experiences show, the institutional frameworks of associations and their supplementary institutions have various shortcomings. These certainly cause frustration for the associates. They also raise doubts about the desirability of association as an alternative to membership.

A first concern is the frequency with which institutions meet. Once each agreement has entered into force, the institutions are quickly established. The association council has always held its inaugural meeting shortly thereafter, usually within one month. One of its first

5.   *OJ* L393, 31 December 1987.

Table 3.2: Examples of Subcommittees of Association Committees

Czech Republic–EC Europe Agreement		EEA
1 Customs Cooperation	I	Free Movement of Goods
2 Transport Issues	II	Free Movement of Capital and
3 Agriculture		Services
4 Approximation of Legislation	III	Free Movement of Persons
5 Science and Technology	IV	Flanking and Horizontal Policies
6 Industrial Standards and Conformity	V	Legal and Institutional Matters
Assessment		
7 Economic Policy Issues		
8 Competition and States Aids		
9 Contact Group on ECSC Matters		

Sources: Mayhew 1998: 59; EFTA 1998.

decisions is normally the adoption of rules of procedure for the association committee. Early on too, association parliamentary committees (APCs), or as they are more commonly called joint parliamentary committees (JPCs), have generally met for the first time.[6] Yet although institutions have been established swiftly, they have not necessarily met with appropriate frequency thereafter. In the case of Greece, during the first four-and-a-half years of its association, the Association Council met on no fewer than 24 occasions, averaging one meeting every ten weeks (Buck 1978: 41). But since those early days of the EEC, the situation has changed dramatically. Association councils meet much less frequently, even when the associations are fully functioning.[7] The EEA Council, for example, has been meeting only twice a year since its creation in 1994. The association councils provided for in the Europe Agreements have been meeting even less frequently. These are required to meet only once a year and so far this has been interpreted literally. Gaps of up to 18 months, if not longer, between some meetings are not

6.   Indeed, in some cases, inaugural meetings have preceded the entry into force of the association agreement. The EC–Hungary APC first met on 26–27 January 1994. Hungary's Europe Agreement entered into force a few days later on 1 February 1994. There have been exceptions, however. Inaugural meetings of the EC–Cyprus and EC–Malta APCs did not take place until 1992!

7.   Where associations have not been fully operational, meetings have understandably become even less frequent. In the case of the EC–Malta association, the association council met on only four occasions during the period of Labour governments in Malta (1971–87).

uncommon. For example, the third meeting of the EU–Poland Association Council was held on 30 April 1997. The next meeting was not held until 10 November 1998. Evidently, logistical factors are responsible: the demands on foreign ministers and the number of individual association councils have increased.

In the absence of frequent meetings of the association council, the effective functioning of the association often relies on the more regular meetings of the association committee. Here, meetings tend to be more frequent. For example, in 1997 the EEA Joint Committee met 12 times. The five sub-committees met a total of 22 times. Yet meetings could be more frequent. In the case of the Europe Agreements, meetings of the individual association committees tend to take place only twice a year. As for the APCs/JPCs, these tend to meet at most once a year. Such a low frequency of meetings does not lead to dynamic institutional links. Given too that decisions relating to the association have to go through the association council, delays between meetings mean that progress can be slow.

The second problem with the institutional framework is the content of meetings. In theory, the institutional framework of any association is designed to ensure the effective functioning of the association and, in the case of the association councils established under the Europe Agreements, promote dialogue on bilateral and international issues of mutual interest. Yet rarely is sufficient time invested in meetings to enable any genuine evaluation, negotiation or dialogue to take place. This can be due, on the one hand, to the fact that meetings tend to be brief. The first meeting of the EU–Hungary Association Council, for example, only lasted half an hour (Dienes-Oehm 1996: 87).[8] Consequently, opportunities for full and frank discussions at ministerial level can be limited. On the other hand, any scope for negotiation is limited by the fact that the EC's position is already the outcome of a negotiation between its Member States. Even when the EC had only six members, this was recognized as a problem. Early on, Greek representatives in the EC–Greece Association Council were often presented with proposals on a 'like it or leave it' basis. Moreover, any EC proposals were often presented only hours before the Association Council met.

---

8. Despite the fact that association is with the EC, the association councils established under the Europe Agreements refer to the EU in their titles. This emphasizes the fact that they do not deal exclusively with EC matters but also cover issues relating to the JHA and CFSP pillars.

If the Greek government wished to consider these, formal discussion had to be delayed until a later meeting.

Fewer complaints are made about association committees. Indeed, Mayhew describes the association committee as the 'workhorse' of Europe Agreements (1998: 54). Such a view is implicit in one early analysis of Hungary's experiences. This concluded that 'the Association Committee, as a real operative institution, played an important role in implementing and in developing the association' (Dienes-Oehm 1996: 88). Yet as Mayhew comments, association committees tend to get heavily involved in fine detail. Hence, 'there is never any consideration of the overall macroeconomic situation or even the real interest of the European Union (not to speak of the interest of Europe)' (1998: 57). Clearly there is a case for the content and length of meetings to be increased. Some compensation is, however, available via APCs and JPCs where the broader context of the association can feature. Meetings provide useful fora for developing a greater understanding of issues between the EC/EU and the associates. Moreover, MEPs have not shied away from using JPCs to draw attention to often sensitive political issues and questions concerning the commitment to democratic reform with the associated state. Yet, as discussion rather than decision-making fora, the impact of these committees on associations is arguably limited. Little attention is paid to their declarations and statements.

A third issue has been decision-making within the association which technically is based on unanimity. Each associate can therefore veto the adoption of any proposed measure. Yet few associates find themselves in a position where exercising the veto is seen as advisable politically. In the case of those associates that see the association as a stepping-stone to membership, refusing to accept a proposed measure, particularly where this involves the adoption of a piece of EC legislation, could be interpreted by the EC/EU as a sign of unwillingness to face up to the requirements of membership and so undermine an associate's accession prospects. This is particularly true at a time when there are numerous other states intent on membership and the EU's capacity to enlarge to include all is limited. Another case is that of the EFTA states participating in the EEA where acceptance of EC legislation and relevant ECJ interpretations is required. To refuse to adopt an EC proposal could result in either the relevant provisions of the EEA being suspended for all EFTA parties or safeguard measures being taken by the EC. Not surprisingly, given the uncertainty of the consequences, political leaders of participating EFTA states have been reluctant to exercise their veto.

A fourth issue to be considered is the impact that associates have on the EC's policy-making process. No associate has ever been granted a role in EC decision-making since participation is reserved for Member States alone. Yet, as noted in the previous chapter, the EEA includes a commitment on the part of the EC to involve its EEA partners in a 'continuous information and consultation process'.[9] Such involvement is crucial given the number of legislative acts which EFTA states participating in the EEA have to adopt. In the period 1994–98, they totalled more than 1700 (see Table 3.3). It is also vital if domestic opposition to the EEA is to be averted. In Norway, the EEA has been attacked for turning the country into a 'fax democracy' where directives are faxed through from Brussels for the Oslo government to implement (Bonde 1998).

Table 3.3: Enlarging the EEA *Acquis*

	EEA Joint Committee decisions	Acts additional to or amending the EEA *acquis*
1994	44	600
1995	75	92
1996	84	89
1997	107	144
1998	122	824
Total	*432*	*1749*

Note: The figures are provisional and include 530 acts contained in the 1994 'additional package' and 644 acts in a new Annex 1 adopted in 1998.

Source: EFTA Secretariat.

What impact officials from the participating EFTA states have had in the decision-shaping process is difficult to gauge. Certainly, there are opportunities to participate in debates, and Norwegian officials do argue that they are being listened to carefully when they attend Commission committee meetings. Early concerns that participation was being kept to a minimum have been partially overcome since it appears

9.   Also of note is the EC's commitment under the 1995 Customs Union Agreement to consult Turkey when drafting legislation affecting the customs union.

that the decision-shaping mechanisms did contribute to a negotiated settlement of a dispute over salmon prices in 1997. That said, Norway's Foreign Minister, Knut Vollebaek has acknowledged that ensuring Norwegian views are taken into account before the EC takes its decisions is 'in itself...no small task and one to which we will have to continue to devote considerable time'. Moreover, the official channels set up under the EEA are not regarded as sufficient. As Vollebaek has pointed out:

> merely being active in Brussels is not enough...the work we do in other European capitals may be at least as important... In order to safeguard our own interests properly, we must ensure that we have close ties with each of the European countries, and this is a time consuming and demanding task.[10]

Vollebaek's predecessor, Tore Godal was more precise:

> During the process of clarifying the Norwegian position on proposals from the Commission that are relevant to the EEA Agreement, we will use the Nordic channels to identify common Nordic interests at the earliest possible stage... This could make it easier to gain acceptance for common Nordic interests in Brussels... With a weakened EFTA pillar [following the EU's 1995 enlargement], we are in a more vulnerable position when conflicts of interest arise.[11]

Clearly, having an audience at committee level provides scant compensation for non-involvement in the adoption of decisions that in all likelihood will be applied to the EEA. Hence, for Norway coaxing neighbouring states into either supporting its interests or recognizing a common Nordic interest is seen as the vital supplement to the formal mechanisms of decision-shaping. For earlier associates such an option was not necessarily available. For example, Greek officials, when faced with the prospect of policy harmonization under the Athens Agreement, found that their influence was almost non-existent. Policy harmonization actually meant alignment with existing and future EC Policy.

The shortcomings with the institutional frameworks set up by associations are plain to see, and they have not necessarily been remedied where the EU has created a supplementary mechanism. A good example is the multilateral framework for dialogue involving CEE states

10. Statement to the Storting on Foreign Policy, Oslo, 22 January 1998 (via http://odin.dep.no/ud/taler/1998/ u980122e.html).

11. Statement to the Storting on Foreign Policy, Oslo, 30 January 1997 (via http://odin.dep.no/ud/taler/97/ 970130e.html).

which was established in part to compensate the *Visegrád* states (the Czech Republic, Hungary, Poland and Slovakia) for the delays in establishing political dialogue given the slow ratification of their Europe Agreements, but also in part to minimize the resourcing implications for the EC/EU of holding several bilateral meetings covering similar issues. A first step came in May 1992 when an initial round of multilateral dialogue between the foreign ministers of the EC Troika and the *Visegrád* countries took place. This was followed in October 1992 by a meeting between EC and *Visegrád* foreign ministers and then a first summit of EC and *Visegrád* heads of government. Then, at Copenhagen in June 1993, the European Council announced the establishment of 'a structured relationship with the institutions of the Union within the framework of a reinforced and extended multilateral dialogue' (*Bull. EC* 6-93: I.3.12). This would involve all CEE states that had signed a Europe Agreement and include regular meetings at the level of Commission and Council Presidents, joint meetings of all heads of government and advisory meetings at Council level. In all, more that 100 meetings were held at ministerial level between 1993 and 1997 (Lippert and Becker 1998: 356). Structured dialogue was also established with Malta and Cyprus in 1995.[12]

Experiences of these multilateral fora and of political dialogue have not been totally positive. Admittedly, the structured dialogue has facilitated discussion of JHA and CFSP matters and provided associates with opportunities to join the EU on common positions in international fora. All the same, while dialogue has been welcomed, Kiss suggests that its contents have 'never offered any opening towards a genuine political cooperation' (1995: 280). Early meetings were often of a 'purely consultative, or advisory' nature, while lower-level contacts remained 'marginal and accidental' with agendas of meetings showing 'signs of automatism'. Similarly, for CEE participants, the dialogue often involved merely the receipt of information rather than an exchange of views. Added to this, meetings tended to be ill-prepared, short (generally limited to one-and-a-half hours), and lacking in continuity and coordination. On the CEE side, the absence of a coordinated position did not improve matters. The *Visegrád* states were particularly

12. The structured dialogue has, however, since been abandoned with the launch of the accession process in 1998 (see p. 109). The structured dialogue with Malta was suspended prior to this in November 1996 following the decision of the incoming Labour government to withdraw Malta's application for EU membership.

frustrated by the widening of the process to include other CEE associates as this made discussions too general and insufficiently focused on their specific needs.

Criticisms of the political dialogue did lead to a reform of procedures in 1995 and an intensification of the contacts. In some areas, experiences of the structured dialogue did improve, notably where it covered the CFSP and the internal market. Top level meetings involving foreign ministers and political leaders also appear to have involved genuine dialogue. In others cases, however, meetings have continued to involve little more than 'boring monologues' from the EU side. There have indeed been occasions where meetings following sessions of the Council of Ministers have consisted of little more than a report of the Council's deliberations. Concerns have also been expressed about the limited progress made with issues when they are passed up from expert to ministerial level. Not surprisingly, criticisms of the organization and content of dialogue persist. Commenting on meetings covering JHA matters, Eisl concludes that the structured dialogue was 'mainly a political forum and has had hardly any concrete effects at an operational level' (1997: 366). Overall, therefore, the experiences were disappointing.

Evidently, the structured dialogue had its weaknesses. In many respects, these were similar to those experienced within the formal institutional framework of associations. Associates are non-Member States and they therefore remain, for the most part, outside the EC's policy- and decision-making institutions and procedures. What dialogue does take place generally depends on the agenda of the EC/EU. Associates have little opportunity to influence the EC/EU and are therefore faced with a simple choice of either maintaining their own position or adapting it to that of the EC/EU. The pressure to adapt is great. Non-adaptation runs the risk of the EC adopting safeguard measures, the relevant area of the association agreement being suspended (as in the case of the EEA), or even membership prospects being compromised.

Trade Relations

A source of even greater disillusionment for some associates has been the impact of the association on trade with the EC. In all cases, the trade provisions of each association agreement have been implemented, and in the cases of Turkey and Cyprus, the trade regime has been upgraded to that of customs union with the EC. Yet associates have been disillusioned on two counts. First, there is the alleged protectionism of the EC. This results from a number of factors including the level of trade concessions contained in the association agreement, the availability and the EC's use of safeguard measures, and the EC's reluctance to grant extra trade concessions during the course of the association. The second source of disillusionment has been the impact of association on trade flows. For all associates, trade with the EC has increased. For the most part, however, increases in trade have been accompanied by a significant worsening in each associate's balance of trade with the EC. Both issues have arisen in the associations created with Turkey, Malta, Cyprus and the CEE states. Greece too experienced a worsening of trade balances.

For the first two associates, Greece and Turkey, a key aim of each association was the creation of a customs union. As noted, however, only the Athens Agreement with Greece originally contained a timetable to effect this. The EC and Turkey did conclude an Additional Protocol in 1970 outlining how a customs union would be achieved, but this did not provide adequate trade concessions in those areas, notably textiles and agricultural goods, where Turkey had a particular export potential. The situation was compounded first in 1974 by the United Kingdom's unilateral measures against Turkish cotton yarn exports, and subsequently in the period 1978–86 by the EC's bans on imports of Turkish clothing products. Moreover, when negotiations later took place on improving market access for such products, the EC was reluctant to meet Turkish requests for fear of having to make similar concessions to other countries. Requests were also unsuccessfully made for permission to protect domestic industry.

The situation regarding trade concessions was exacerbated by the erosion of their real value as the EC granted similar concessions to other countries via its General System of Preferences (GSP), the Lomé Agreement (1975), and the Integrated Mediterranean Programme. Turkey naturally complained that this undermined the privileged relationship created by the association. The prospect of enlargement to include Greece, Spain and Portugal gave further cause for concern. Through accession, these countries would gain automatic free access to the EC market and therefore a distinct advantage over Turkey, particularly in important sectors such as textiles and agricultural goods. As one Turkish Foreign Ministry official argued in 1979, if trade concessions were to be eroded any further, then Turkey would be paying the bill for enlargement (Keskin 1979: 70-71). The EC's response, not surprisingly, was to argue that it could not allow its external trade policy to be determined by an associate. Nevertheless, Turkey was granted extra concessions in 1980. Initially, these did provide Turkish producers with greater preferential access to the EC market. However, by 1986, other Mediterranean countries had also been granted the same access as compensation for the EC's Iberian enlargement. Once again any sense that the association provided a privileged relationship was undermined, a feeling that persisted into the 1990s. With the move to customs union in 1996, Turkey's grounds for complaint were reduced. Trade in all manufactured goods including textiles was to be barrier-free. Provision also exists for Turkey's gradual adoption of the CAP thus creating free trade in agricultural goods. In the meantime, there was a commitment to improve preferential access to the EC market. A first deal on improved access was concluded in early 1998.

Clearly, Turkey struggled for much of the first three decades of its association to obtain the fullest possible access to the EC market. Arguably, Turkey needed extra concessions in order to halt and reverse the trade deficit with the EC which developed as the association was put in place and trade liberalized. Greece too experienced a worsening situation in its balance of trade with the EC, even though exports increased with association. During the period 1962–75, growth in Greek exports to the EC stood at 21.1% per annum compared with a rate of 4.2% per annum for the pre-association period. By 1978, 46% of Greek exports were going to the EC(6) and 51% to the EC(9).[13] The situation regarding Turkey was less encouraging. Figures covering the period up until 1970 show no exceptional increases in Turkish exports other than for hazelnuts. Any growth in exports tended to reflect a normal rate of growth rather than a response to trade concessions from the EC. The impact of trade preferences granted by the EC appears to have been negligible. Moreover, the rates at which Turkish exports to the EC increased were generally below those for other countries.

As for the overall balance of trade with the EC, Greece and Turkey had similar initial experiences: deficits increased. In the case of Turkey, a deficit of US$ 5 million in 1965 had grown to US$ 121 million within three years. By the second half of the 1970s, it was increasing at alarming rates, rising in the period 1973–75 from US$ 544 million to

13. Figures taken from Perdikis (1981: 103) and Mitsos (1983: 111).

US$ 1528 million. As noted below, responsibility for such rises cannot be attributed solely, if at all, to the association. Turkey's domestic economic policy did not facilitate exploitation of the trade opportunities available. Yet, a worsening trade deficit with the EC so soon after concluding the Additional Protocol in 1970, which was supposed to bring trade benefits, could not but lead to disillusionment with the association. The deficit did subsequently narrow as a result of significant increases in the value of Turkish exports to the EC. All the same, it still stood at US$ 678 million in 1985 (Akagül 1987: 5).

Such deficits can be used to cast doubt on the contribution of association to the balanced development of trade between the EC and Greece and Turkey. Any such doubts are reinforced by the conclusions drawn from analyses of Greece's economic performance in the 1960s. Increases in trade could not necessarily be attributed to the association. They took place at a time of domestic economic boom, technological advances, increased specialization and a reversal in the rapid decline in exports in the late 1950s. The association's contribution to trade creation was undoubtedly very small (Tsoukalis 1981; Hitiris 1972: 154; Pomfret 1986: 49-50). In the case of Turkey, the contribution was seemingly limited too. Here, however, domestic policy decisions did not create a climate in which the association could flourish. Only limited empirical evidence exists in support of the argument that insufficient trade concessions were primarily responsible for the trade deficit. Rather, much of the blame can be attributed to the lack of policy coordination if not contradictory policies in Turkey in the 1970s—a situation previously hidden by the economic success of the 1960s. The Foreign Ministry, responsible for all negotiations with the EC, favoured integration through gradual trade liberalization towards a customs union and the pursuit of an outward-looking economic policy promoting a more open, modern and competitive economy. By contrast, for much of the first two decades of the association, the State Planning Organization (SPO) ensured that successive Turkish governments pursued a policy centred on an essentially inward-looking and protected, if not closed, economy with economic and industrial development policies based on import-substitution, protection and heavy state control.[14] That the association should fail to bring desired results during the 1970s in particular is hardly surprising.

14. The apparent contradiction here between the provisions of the association agreement and the policy pursued by the Turkish government was acknowledged by

Since the mid-1980s, Turkish governments have adopted an economic policy based on trade liberalization and less state planning. This has been accompanied by increased exports to the EC market with average levels in the period 1990–94 being double the annual average for 1980–89. In more recent years, the annual level of exports to the EC has exceeded US$ 11 billion, but the trade deficit has still increased. By 1995 it had reached US$ 5790 million. While running a trade deficit with the EC may be considered desirable for a developing economy such as Turkey, its persistence can lead people to view the association as providing disproportionate benefits to the EU. Certainly, the prospect of a customs union led to concerns being voiced about increased competition. Such fears were arguably justified. During the first year of the customs union, Turkey's trade deficit with the EU rose sharply to $US 11,228 million (Akagül 1998: 365). To many, the association appeared to be benefiting the EU rather than Turkey.

An examination of the EC's trade relations with Malta and Cyprus during association reveals similar sentiments. In both cases, there was a marked increase in the value of trade. In the period 1970–85, Maltese exports to the EC increased thirteenfold from M£ 9 million to M£ 117 million. By 1987 the EC(10) was receiving 71% of Malta's exports. Goods from the EC(10) now accounted for 65.78% of imports.[15] Much of the increase could be attributed to the association. It was accompanied by a period of rapid expansion in manufacturing exports based on industries whose growth was fuelled by foreign investment (Pomfret 1982: 241). The association did not, however, promote agricultural exports—a situation not improved by the erosion of trade preferences. Moreover, Malta was experiencing a widening visible trade deficit with the EC. During the first 11 years of the association, this rose from a low of ECU 63 million in 1972 to ECU 273 million in 1982. The situation did not improve in the 1980s. For much of the decade, the value of Maltese exports to the EC was half that of imports from the EC. Although much of this deficit was covered by invisible earnings from tourism, the fact that association was accompanied by a trade deficit

the SPO in a report issued in 1972. This argued that the implementation of the provisions of the Additional Protocol would be impossible given the wording of the constitution. By pursuing relations with the EC, Turkey would have to abandon its economic principles, its economic system, and its methods (Steinbach 1977: 100).

15. Figures taken from Rossi (1986: 33) and Maltese EC Directorate (1990: 207-209).

suggested an imbalance in benefits. By the mid-1990s, the deficit was averaging over ECU 550 million per annum.[16]

As in the case of Turkey, any evaluation of the association must include consideration of domestic economic policy in Malta. Undoubtedly, this failed to create an economic climate where full advantage could be taken of the association. Under Labour governments, the policies pursued were in direct contradiction with the association's aims. The fourth development plan (1973–79), for example, placed considerable emphasis on direct government involvement at the expense of private sector initiatives. The plans also focused domestic production on the home market and afforded domestic producers protection from competition abroad. Not surprisingly, Maltese industrialists supported the government's opposition to moves in the direction of customs union. Even after economic liberalization post-1987, the Maltese economy was characterized by extensive protection. Much progress was needed before Malta could comply with the rules governing the internal market. Domestic policy for much of the association ensured only limited progress in the economic integration of Malta with the EC.

Evaluations of Cyprus's early experiences of associations draw similar conclusions. There is little evidence to suggest that new markets were opening up or that industrial exports were being encouraged to any great extent. Tsardanidis observes that in the period up to 1980 association 'had no favourable results for Cyprus' trade with the EC' (1988: 274). Trade flows did increase. Yet whereas Cypriot imports from the EC in the period 1973–82 increased by 319%, Cypriot exports to the EC only grew by 44.7%. Moreover, the importance of the EC as one of Cyprus's trading partners actually decreased. By 1980 the proportion of trade going to the EC(6) plus the United Kingdom had more than halved to 28.2% since 1972. Developments in Cyprus–EC trade flatly contradicted the widespread conviction that exports to the EC market would significantly increase. Once again, the reasons for this do not necessarily lie in the association. Some of the initial decline in trade could be attributed to EC quotas. Yet the limited competitiveness of Cypriot products and the lack of effective marketing were of greater significance. A further factor was Cyprus's geographical location. Proximity to and long-standing familiarity with Middle East markets coupled with the export opportunities created by the collapse

16. Calculated from EC Commission (1999).

of Lebanese industry ensured that trade prior to the early 1980s became focused on the Arab world. Such factors also account for Cyprus's worsening visible trade deficit with the EC. Initially, this rose from Cy£ 28.0 million in 1975 to Cy£ 73.9 million in 1977. By 1983, it had increased to Cy£ 253 million. The deficit would remain. By 1989 it stood at Cy£ 393 million. Invisible earnings, especially from tourism, did help reduce the overall deficit. All the same, by 1997 it stood at CY£ 730 million.[17]

The experiences of the EC's first four European associates in terms of trade relations are clearly mixed. The same can be said for CEE associates. They too were expected to benefit from the trade provisions of their associations. Indeed, early Europe Agreements gave the respective CEE producers a significant advantage over their competitors from Mediterranean and other East European countries. Yet although the EC has reduced import tariffs and abolished quantitative restrictions at a faster rate than the associates, justifiable criticism has been levelled against the EC for its failure to grant the associates sufficient market access, particularly in those areas (e.g. agriculture, textiles, steel) where the CEE associates, initially at least, enjoyed a competitive advantage. Such access has been of vital importance for the economic and political stability and development of the CEE associates. This was particularly so given the collapse of trade among the former members of the CMEA, notably with the USSR, and the subsequent trade dependence of the associates on the EC.

The criticisms of the Europe Agreements' trade provisions take a variety of forms. First, while the objective of establishing free trade asymmetrically has been praised, the scope of the concessions has been attacked. Indeed, Gowan argues that the concessions represented only a marginal improvement on existing rules under the GSP, and that the value of the asymmetry would later be halved by the outcome of the Uruguay GATT round (1993: 13). Secondly, the agreements can be criticized for effectively forcing the CEE associates to adopt protectionist trade policies. In several instances, they were obliged to raise import tariffs. Thirdly, the EC has been criticized heavily for the slow and drawn out manner in which it agreed to open up its most sensitive markets. Indeed, because of CAP principles and opposition from EC farmers, free trade in agricultural goods is not even envisaged under association. Similarly, access is determined more on the basis of imme-

17. The figures are calculated from EC Commission (1998a: 5).

diate reciprocity than according to asymmetry. Concessions, according to Messerlin, were essentially 'embryonic and uncertain' (1992: 117). Hence, Winters refers to the EC's approach as 'managed liberalization' (1993: 122). To have granted immediate access would, however, have required substantial CAP reform for which EC political will was lacking. With regard to other sensitive products, the slow rate of liberalization has been harshly criticized given the asymmetric value of trade in these areas. Whereas in 1992 sensitive products made up 33–51% of *Visegrád* exports to the EC, they accounted for only 2% of total EC imports of sensitive goods. In the case of Hungary, doubts have been expressed as to whether the EC's concessions will actually provide real support to the reform process (Hantke 1995: 118). Rollo and Smith suggested that both the EC and the CEE associates would gain substantially if the agricultural exports of the latter were granted free access to the EC market (1993). Similarly, gains would be made if free trade were established for all sensitive goods.

Furthermore, the Europe Agreements' anti-dumping and safeguard provisions also threaten trade and could deter would-be investors. On the former, fears have been realized. Pressure from domestic EC producers has ensured use of the provisions. Measures were introduced in 1992 against imports of steel, mainly from Czechoslovakia, followed later by a one-month general ban on meat imports from 18 CEE countries in April 1993. While these reinforced perceptions of the EC as protectionist, they also discouraged investment and slowed the pace of restructuring in CEE countries. Also, provision for anti-dumping measures would appear to be excessive given the requirement that the CEE associates adopt EC competition law. As Winters argues, CEE producers 'suffer potential double jeopardy—if competition law doesn't get them, anti-dumping will' (1992: 26). Finally, doubts were initially raised as to whether the timetable for CEE tariff reductions would be long enough to enable the economies to become competitive, particularly given the slow progress many industrial sectors in the EC have taken to restructure.

Such criticisms have clearly highlighted factors that could limit the potential trade gains from the Europe Agreements. Yet both official and academic studies have argued that the CEE countries will gain economically from the Europe Agreements (Adamiec 1993: 13-14; Mastropasqua and Rolli 1994). Indeed, the effect of the agreements in trade terms seems to have been positive. Since 1989 EU–CEE trade has been dynamic. Figures for the CEE(6) in the period 1989–95 show an average per annum increase of more than 20% for both imports and exports.[18] The same is true for the CEE(10) in 1994–95. Moreover, there has been a substantial reorientation of CEE trade towards the EU. By 1994, the EU market accounted for more than 50% of exports from the CEE(6). Consequently, it seems that the Europe Agreements have resulted in trade creation.

However, before too much credit can be attributed to association, several points suggest that the impact of the Europe Agreements has been less than would ideally have been the case. The significant reorientation of CEE countries' trade towards the EU market, particularly in the period 1989–91 cannot be attributed to the Europe Agreements as their trade provisions did not enter into force until March 1992. Rather, increased CEE exports were the result of a unique German import boom and the extension of the EC's GSP to the CEE countries in 1990 (Inotai 1994: 147-48). In any case, the high figures for increased trade flows, at least early on, reflect the low base from which trade grew. There can be little doubt that trade liberalization, while benefiting the CEE economies, has also benefited the EU. Indeed, EU exports to the CEE countries have generally grown at a faster rate than CEE exports to the EU. Hence, and in common with all other associations except the EEA, the effect of trade liberalization on most CEE countries has been either the creation or worsening of a trade deficit with the EU. In the period 1994–96, for example, Poland's visible trade deficit with the EU(12) worsened from ECU 1722 million to ECU 6680 million. Moreover, growth in CEE trade with the EU has not been constant. Indeed, in 1993 and 1996 (with the exception of Estonia, Latvia, Lithuania and, in 1993, Romania) growth was in single figures, often less than one-third of the previous year's rate, and in some cases negative. Finally, despite the increase in trade flows, there has been no major restructuring of CEE countries' foreign trade. There is still a heavy reliance on textiles, iron, steel and machinery (Mayhew 1998: 80-81).

Admittedly, the poor export performance of CEE associates can in part be blamed on recession in the EU. Equally, economies in transition

18. The CEE(6) includes Bulgaria, the Czech Republic, Hungary, Poland, Romania and Slovakia). The CEE(10) is the CEE(6) plus Estonia, Latvia, Lithuania and Slovenia. The figures are taken from Grabbe and Hughes (1998) and Mayhew (1998).

are almost certain to experience trade deficits as they import machinery and technology to modernize their economies and increase their output potential. Added to this, individual countries' performances will be affected by the progress they have made with economic reform. To blame the EC and the Europe Agreements alone for trade imbalances would be misleading. Association does provide better access to EC markets.

The reaction of the CEE countries, especially the *Visegrád* 4, to what were perceived as the limited trade benefits from the Europe Agreements was to call on the EC to grant additional trade concessions. The EC responded by endorsing an acceleration of the trade liberalization timetable, particularly with regard to agriculture and other sensitive areas. Hence, additional protocols were signed on 21–22 December 1993 with Bulgaria, the Czech Republic, Hungary, Poland and Romania.[19] The remaining CEE countries would have the concessions incorporated into their as yet unsigned free trade or Europe Agreements. As a consequence of this, criticisms of the EU's position regarding market access decreased. They also abated owing to the fact that since 1 January 1996 all CEE associates have enjoyed duty- and quota-free access to the EU market for textiles and ECSC goods. Also, since 1 July 1997 pan-European cumulative rules of origin have been in place. All this has helped improve export opportunities, although access to the EU market for agricultural produce remains limited.

Financial Assistance

A fifth area in which the experiences of association can be assessed is in terms of the financial assistance made available. In the cases of Greece and Turkey their original association agreements were accompanied by financial protocols. Associations established with Malta and Cyprus also involved the conclusion, albeit once the association had been established, of such agreements. By the time that the CEE states came to negotiate the Europe Agreements, however, financial protocols were no longer seen as an integral part of association. Even so, aid was made available to the new associates via other mechanisms. As for the EEA Agreement, this is association with a difference. Here, the associates create a financial mechanism to assist the EC in reducing the economic and social disparities within the EEA.

19. *OJ* L25, 29 January 1994.

In the case of the EC's first association, that with Greece, the experiences of financial assistance were limited. Of the US$ 125 million made available in the protocol attached to the association agreement, only US$ 75 million had been made available to Greece prior to the 'freezing' of the association, and therefore financial aid, in 1967–74. For the Greeks, the amount of assistance received was far too small and arguably of marginal use. A second financial protocol to the value of ECU 280 million was later agreed in February 1977 and rapidly committed.

The Greek reaction to the amount of aid received was not dissimilar to that which would later come from Turkish circles. Indeed, Turkey argued on various occasions that the amounts made available (see Table 3.4) consistently fell short of those requested. Although the US$ 195 million agreed under the second protocol was US$ 20 million more than under its predecessor this was considerably less than the US$ 900 million sought. Yet accusations of miserliness levelled against the EC were often misplaced. The absorption capacity of the Turkish economy was limited and difficulties involved in investing money in private enterprise meant that less than one-third of the first financial protocol had been utilized by the end of 1968. Given such a situation, there appeared little reason to make vast sums of money available. Nevertheless, the desired amount of financial aid remained considerably higher than that which the EC was willing to grant. Indeed, the ECU 300 million made available under the third financial protocol in 1976 was less than one-third of the amount being sought. Likewise, the ECU 600 million package of grants and concessionary loans contained in the fourth financial protocol in 1981 fell considerably short of the US$ 7 billion requested in 1978. Whether the economic justification for more aid existed is doubtful. Yet to critics of the association, the apparent miserliness of the EC suggested that its commitment to the economic development and ultimate accession of Turkey was lacking. Indeed, although the ECU 600 million compared favourably with the amount granted to Egypt and Algeria, it was considerably less, on a *per capita* basis, than that granted to Tunisia and Morocco (Lycourgos 1994: 301-302). Indeed, estimates of the level of aid received in the period 1964–92 show that Turkey received the equivalent of 0.1% of its GDP. This compares poorly with Yugoslavia (1.25%) and Tunisia (0.4%), neither of which were due to expose domestic producers to full competition from EC competitors through the establishment of a customs

Table 3.4: Financial Assistance to Associates: Turkey, Malta and Cyprus

	Turkey			Malta			Cyprus		
	Period	Signed	Total	Period	Signed	Total	Period	Signed	Total
First	1964–69	1963	175.0	1976–83	1976	26.0	1979–84	1977	30.0
Second	1973–76	1970	195.0	1983–88	1986	38.0	1984–88	1983	44.0
Third	1979–81	1977	310.0	1988–93	1989	29.5	1989–95	1989	62.0
Fourth	1981–	1981	600.0	1995–98	1995	45.0	1995–98	1995	74.0
MEDA*	1996–99	1995	375						

Notes: Figures are in million ECUs except for those relating to Turkey for 1964–76. These are in US$ million.

* The MEDA programme provides aid to finance the implementation of the Euro-Mediterranean partnership. It is designed to replace existing financial protocols.

union with the EC (Balkir 1993: 129). The apparent imbalance here certainly reflects both the freezing of aid following the military coup in 1980 and Greece's refusal to agree to the fourth financial protocol. Indeed, the protocol has still to be approved. Moreover, although the customs union agreement of 1995 was supposed to herald a new era in relations, there is still no unanimous agreement over the new financial regulation. Association for Turkey is not bringing the envisaged benefits through financial assistance.

Maltese experiences have been more encouraging. The fact that in trade terms the association did not prove wholly beneficial has been offset in part by the fact that financial aid was received. Such aid during the period 1976–98 amounted to more than ECU 128 million (see Table 3.4). This was used to promote the social and economic development of the island. In the case of Cyprus too, the aid received did contribute to the development of various valuable infrastructure projects. It was not, however, enough to compensate for the negative results of increased competition from EC producers. That said, one Cypriot survey does conclude that the importance of the third financial protocol (1989–95) with respect to the restructuring and modernization of the Cypriot economy was 'considerable'. Funds made available, while not that impressive, 'unequivocally constitute a decisive aid' for the Cypriot economy (Euroconsult 1991: 68).

As far as the Europe Agreements are concerned, there are no financial protocols. They do, however, provide for three types of financial assistance: PHARE, loans from the European Investment Bank (EIB), and temporary financial assistance to support stabilization and structural adjustment. None of these forms of assistance was created by the Europe Agreement. Each was available before the first agreements were signed. Hence, in the case of Hungary, Martonyi notes that 'the Europe Agreement neither significantly improved nor worsened the conditions, the volume and the mechanisms of the financial assistance' (1996: 27). Yet aid has been forthcoming. The ten CEE associates received ECU 4442 million in PHARE aid in 1990–96. During a similar period (1990–95), the EIB also made available loans to the value of ECU 3645 million.[20] What impact such assistance will have is difficult to gauge. Suffice to say that when it launched *Agenda 2000* the Commission recognized that more aid would be needed if the economies of CEE

20. Figures taken from Grabbe and Hughes (1998: 39) and Mayhew (1998: 157).

states were to be prepared for accession. It proposed, from 2000 onwards and on an annual basis, structural assistance of ECU 1 billion, ECU 500 million in the form of agricultural aid, and an increase in annual support via PHARE of ECU 1.5 billion (EC Commission 1997a: III).

Although each association has been accompanied by some form of financial assistance from the EC to the associate, there is little evidence to suggest that the amounts of aid have been particularly generous. Most associates note the benefits of the assistance. Yet few if any would argue that the amounts received were adequate. Whether the same can be said for the EU recipients of assistance under the EEA financial mechanism is difficult to assess because the beneficiaries also receive the bulk of aid made available through the EC's own structural funds. However, there are likely to be few complaints since the amount of assistance available through grants and loans is not insignificant. For the period 1994–98, the financial mechanism consisted of ECU 2000 million (see Table 3.5).

Table 3.5: EEA Financial Mechanism: 1994–98 (commitments as of 31 December 1997)

	Grants		Loans		Overall
	Committed (MECU*)	Uncommitted (MECU)	Committed (MECU)	Uncommitted (MECU)	share (%)
Greece	64.7	56.8	299.8	64.7	24.3
Ireland	35.5	—	40.0	66.5	7.1
Northern Ireland	8.0	3.0	—	33.0	2.2
Portugal	52.3	52.7	260.6	54.4	221.0
Spain	213.5	13.5	651.7	29.3	45.4
Total	*374.0*	*126.0*	*1252.1*	*247.9*	*100.0*

* Million ECUs.

Source: EFTA 1998: 55-57.

Cooperation

The actual amount of cooperation that can be developed in an association obviously depends on what provision exists for such, and how well the association functions. Given the history of the early associations, it should come as no surprise that very little cooperation between the EC and its European associates took place prior to the 1990s.

In the case of Greece, the first five years of its association tended to be characterized by a sense of misplaced optimism early on. Nothing spectacular was happening with the association and early enthusiasm was waning. Indeed, as noted above (p. 76), by 1968 there was open talk of 'friction' in the relationship. Such a climate was not conducive to cooperation. Furthermore, with the freezing of the association following the Colonels' coup in 1967 until 1974, no cooperation could take place. Similarly, it was difficult to envisage at this time any co-operation taking place between the EC and Turkey. The Additional Protocol had been signed in 1970, yet relations were soon to experience the disenchantment and malaise of the 1970s. Domestic instability in Turkey and economic recession in Europe were also hardening Turkish attitudes against the EC. Added to this, the military takeover in Turkey in September 1980 resulted in the association being effectively frozen until 1985. The only cooperation was communication on EPC matters (Kramer 1988: 84-111). As for Malta and Cyprus, their association agreements did not actually envisage any cooperation. This is not to say that none could take place, particularly once the second stage had been negotiated. Yet here too there was little prospect of cooperation. In the case of Malta, the Mintoff governments from 1971–84 effectively turned their back on the EC and the association. Cooperation was nei-ther sought nor desired. Cyprus, however, was keen to negotiate the second stage of the association, but the EC's reluctance to further rela-tions given the de facto division of the island meant that no significant progress was made until the mid-1980s.

From the mid-1980s onwards, relations with Malta and Cyprus did improve and, as a consequence, cooperation did develop. A first step, as already noted, was the introduction of political dialogue in 1988. Later in the 1990s, the two associates became participants, along with Turkey, in the Euro-Mediterranean Partnership. This involves coopera-tion in areas such as technology and industry, small and medium-sized enterprises, joint action on the environment, and measures to combat illegal immigration and drug trafficking. Added to this, both associates have participated in EC programmes covering education, research and development, the environment, transport and tourism.

Turning to the EEA Agreement, given its coverage (see pp. 51-52), the fact that implementation has been accompanied by significant levels of cooperation should cause little surprise. Indeed, as far as the EEA is concerned, participating EFTA states have become involved in more than 20 EC programmes and action plans covering research, information services, education, training, youth, employment, social policy, small and medium-sized enterprises, the audio-visual sector, culture and energy.

The same is not necessarily true of the Europe Agreements. Indeed, one senior Commission official dealing with the CEE countries, has argued that the titles on economic and cultural cooperation in the agreements are 'simply long wish-lists for future cooperation' and that the articles contained within them are 'likely to remain unused and unloved for reasons of resource limitation and substance' (Mayhew 1998: 131). Several of the areas are covered by activities carried out under PHARE rather than under the Europe Agreements. These include cross-border cooperation programmes concerning transport, the environment and JHA matters. In addition, most CEE associates have since 1997 participated in educational and youth (Socrates, Leonardo, Youth for Europe), environmental (LIFE) and energy (SAVE) programmes. Added to this, *Agenda 2000* proposed opening up to CEE associated a broad range of EC programmes covering education, training, research, culture, the environment, small and medium-sized enterprises, and the internal market (EC Commission 1997a: IV.3.b). The fact that these were proposals emphasized the fact that cooperation is only really beginning to be developed. Any evaluation of its contribution to the associations would be premature.

Shifting the Purpose of Association: The Question of Membership

The discussion so far suggests that experiences of association have been far less positive than originally anticipated. Not every association has functioned effectively and there is clear evidence that the decision-making realities of association have created political difficulties for associates. Added to this, many associates have been frustrated by EC protectionism and as a result have become somewhat disillusioned with their relations with the EC/EU. Interest in association has not though been entirely lost. In part this reflects the fact that the purpose of many associations has shifted. For those associates intent on acceding to the EU, their associations have been reoriented towards eventual membership. This is true of the associations with Cyprus and the CEE countries. It is also, albeit less explicitly, the case with Malta.

In the case of Cyprus, the reorientation of the association towards membership preparation has been a reaction to the Cypriot government's 1990 application for EC membership. In its opinion, the Commission proposed using 'all the instruments available under the Association Agreement to contribute to the economic, social and political transition of Cyprus towards integration with the Community' (1993a: 49). The reference to 'integration with' rather than 'membership of' was arguably deliberate. The Commission clearly had no desire to proceed towards membership with the island still divided. Nevertheless, in June 1994, the European Council at Corfu dropped the precondition of a solution to the division of the island and announced that Cyprus would be involved in the first round of enlargement negotiations after the 1996 Intergovernmental Conference (IGC) (*Bull. EU* 6-94: I.11). Then, in March 1995, having re-examined the membership application, the Council agreed in principle to begin accession negotiations six months after the IGC.[21] At the same time, it was agreed that a strategy for Cypriot accession, including structured dialogue, would be developed within the framework of the association. The Cypriot government's enthusiastic response was accompanied by suggestions that the completion of the customs union might even be accelerated. Details of the structured dialogue were subsequently agreed at a meeting of the Association Council on 12 June 1995. At the same time, a fourth financial protocol worth ECU 74 million for the period (1995–98) was signed. Evidently, the association was viewed now as only a preparatory stage towards membership. This was confirmed in December 1997 when the European Council at Luxembourg endorsed the recommendation of the Commission in *Agenda 2000* (published in July 1997) that accession negotiations with Cyprus be opened in spring 1998. A specific pre-accession strategy for Cyprus was agreed and with the launch of negotiations in March 1998, Cyprus appeared to be set firmly on the path of membership. The days of association seemed numbered.

21. The announcement was made in exchange for Greek acceptance of a customs union agreement with Turkey. The decision did not, however, appear in the published minutes of the relevant Council meeting (*Council of the European Union Press Release*, 5221/95, 6 March 1995). The Greek Foreign Minister had earlier threatened that the Greek parliament would not ratify the Accession Treaty with Austria, Finland, Norway and Sweden unless the EU committed itself to opening membership negotiations with Cyprus (*Agence Europe*, 6 April 1994: 3).

For Malta, had the Labour Party not won the election of October 1996, then it too could have been in the same position as Cyprus in March 1998. This reflected the fact that the Nationalist Party government was as keen on membership as its Cypriot counterpart. Moreover, there was little enthusiasm for the association. A report from the Maltese government's EC Directorate argued in 1990 that a customs union (i.e. moving to the second stage of the association) would have 'no attraction, whether political or economical [*sic*] for Malta' and would 'only impose certain unnecessary burdens...without deriving any of the advantages to be reaped by membership' (Maltese EC Directorate 1990: 366). The Maltese government applied for membership in July 1990. In doing so, it sought to ensure that Malta was afforded similar if not better treatment to Cyprus by the EC. The EC's initial response came in June 1992 when the European Council at Lisbon announced that Malta would not be included in the next enlargement round but that relations would be developed and strengthened 'by building on the association agreements and [the] application for membership and by developing the political dialogue' (*Bull. EC* 6-92: I.4). The Commission's opinion on Malta's application then advocated opening accession negotiations once the island's economy had become more open and competitive. In the meantime, the Commission proposed offering EC assistance in identifying and assessing priority reforms, particularly relating to the necessary overhaul of the Maltese economy's regulatory and operations systems, and developing an intense dialogue on the nature and the timetable of the reform process and preparations for integration with the EC (EC Commission 1993b: 44-48). Although no explicit mention was made of promoting relations within the context of the association, the Council later advocated using 'all the instruments offered by the Association Agreement' (*Agence Europe* 4–5 October 1993: 7). However, the next meeting of the Association Council did not take place until 12 June 1995, more than three years after the previous meeting.

Once the European Council at its Corfu Summit in June 1994 stated that Malta and Cyprus would be involved in the next set of enlargement negotiations (*Bull. EU* 6-94: I.11), Commission and Council endorsement of Malta's economic reform programme in March 1995 further improved the island's membership prospects. A greater boost came with the Council's announcement on 10 April 1995 that accession negotiations would begin six months after the IGC had been concluded.

Details of the structured dialogue, along with a fourth financial protocol worth ECU 45 million for the period (1995–98), were subsequently agreed by the Association Council in June 1995.[22] Such developments clearly suggested that the future of the association was limited. Malta was evidently moving towards membership.

Yet the Labour Party government that was elected in October 1996 had other ideas. It froze the 1990 membership application and sought to renegotiate and strengthen existing ties on the basis of a free trade zone. The EU responded by accommodating Maltese wishes. Hence, the Commission ignored Malta in its *Agenda 2000* proposals concerning enlargement and proposed establishing a free trade area. Not surprisingly, Malta did not receive an invitation to participate in the accession process launched in March 1998. The island's relations with the EU seemed to be based firmly on the association. Initially, at least, this would remain the case even after the Nationalist Party returned again to power in September 1998. The new government immediately reactivated the application for membership in the hope of being allowed to catch up with those states already involved in negotiations. However, eager not to see unravel an earlier deal in which countries should be invited to negotiate accession, the EU Council of Ministers avoided responding positively to the Maltese government's move. It simply requested that the Commission update its 1993 opinion on Malta's membership application. This was conveniently delayed until after the Vienna Summit of the European Council in December 1998. For the time being, the association remained.

The failure of the EU to include Malta in the accession negotiations launched in March 1998 meant that Malta found itself in a position not dissimilar to some of the CEE associates (i.e. Bulgaria, Latvia, Lithuania, Slovakia and Romania). They too are intent on EU membership. But, like Malta, they are not formally negotiating accession while their associations with the EC are, at least officially, now firmly focused on facilitating their entry into the EU. This represents a significant reformulation of the key strategic objective of the Europe Agreements. Having originally been viewed as sui generis agreements, they have now arguably become stepping-stones to membership.

This reorientation of the Europe Agreements began even before the first ones had entered into force. New initiatives placed the associations

---

22. *EC–Malta Association: The Association Council Press Release*, CE-M 603/95, 12 June 1995.

within a wider process which would relatively quickly become focused on the future accession of the CEE associates to the EU. The first major step in this direction came with the announcement by the European Council at Copenhagen in June 1993 that 'the associated countries of Central and Eastern Europe that so desire shall become members of the European Union' (*Bull. EC* 6-93: I.23). While such a statement did not change the legal substance of the Europe Agreements, it did signal a clear political reorientation of EU strategy towards the CEE states. Moreover, this reorientation implied a reinterpretation, albeit not made explicit at the time, of the associations being created. They would become 'a kind of pre-basis for possible future membership' (Müller-Graff 1997: 35).

The reorientation was confirmed a year later when the Commission published its proposed strategy for preparing CEE states for accession. Significantly, they both had the same main title: 'The Europe Agreements and beyond'. Association was clearly being viewed as a step in the direction of membership. Indeed, the Commission argued that the Europe Agreements provided:

> a common framework for diverse forms of cooperation and integration [which is] flexible and dynamic, permitting the intensification of co-operation and integration...appropriate...for developing a strategy with a view to preparing for accession (EC Commission 1994a: 1).

It added that it was 'crucial to exploit the full potential of the Europe Agreements and to build upon them in preparation for enlargement' (EC Commission 1994a: 4). The Commission's follow-up communication also stressed the need to make full use of the bases for cooperation in the Europe Agreements (EC Commission 1994b).

However, when the European Council launched the pre-accession strategy at Essen in December 1994, the Europe Agreements did not provide the main focus. Rather, they were to complement other elements. These included a new 'structured relationship' involving additional multilateral meetings between the EU and CEE states aimed at encouraging mutual trust and addressing topics of common interest. The key element, however, was 'preparation of the associated states for integration into the internal market of the Union' (*Bull. EU* 12-94: I.13). While maximum use would be made of the Europe Agreements, it was clear that they now provided only one element of EU relations with the CEE countries. This was confirmed when the Commission in May 1995 published its White Paper, 'Preparation of the Associated

Countries of Central and Eastern Europe for Integration into the Internal Market of the Union'. This is essentially a guide for CEE countries on the process of adapting domestic legislation to the EC *acquis* governing the internal market. In total, the White Paper details 23 areas, ranging from the free movement of capital to consumer protection, where the CEE countries would eventually have to align domestic legislation to that of the EC. In addition, it sets out which administrative and technical structures are necessary to assure the effective implementation and enforcement of legislation. To assist in all this, provision is also made for EC technical assistance via the establishment of the Technical Assistance Information Exchange Office (TAIEX) in Brussels.

Although not legally binding, the White Paper created a road-map of sorts towards membership. In placing the emphasis on the CEE countries themselves to prepare for membership, the White Paper did appear, however, to marginalize the Europe Agreements in this process. Association Councils would merely receive reports (EC Commission 1995: 5.3 and 5.9). This is not to say that the Europe Agreements lost all importance. Clearly, given the White Paper's focus on the internal market, it did not cover certain areas dealt with in the Europe Agreements (e.g. fisheries, statistics, small and medium-sized enterprises, cooperation in the fight against drug abuse). Similarly, the basic requirements governing competition policy and the basis for trade in agricultural products are laid down in the Europe Agreements. That said, the Europe Agreements and association were clearly only one element in a wider pre-accession strategy.

The next step towards membership for the CEE associates came in December 1995 when the European Council at Madrid called on the Commission to 'expedite preparation of its opinions on the [membership] applications' of CEE countries (*Bull. EU* 12-95: I.25). This was followed in July 1997 with the publication of *Agenda 2000* and the Commission's opinions on each of the ten CEE applications for membership (EC Commission 1997b). These opinions link progress with association to a state's eligibility for membership, and examine the extent to which the associates have fulfilled their obligations under the Europe Agreements.[23] Yet in determining eligibility greater emphasis

23. Whereas some states were deemed to have made either 'significant efforts' (Bulgaria, Latvia, Lithuania and Romania) or 'serious efforts' (Estonia) to comply with their obligations, Poland and the Czech Republic were considered to have

was given to assessing the CEE states' implementation of the recommendations contained in the 1995 White Paper. The significance of the association to the membership prospects of individual CEE states appeared limited.

Since *Agenda 2000* was launched, however, the role of the associations established by the Europe Agreements does appear to have increased, albeit only marginally. All ten CEE associates have concluded so-called 'accession partnerships' as part of a reinforced accession strategy. The purpose of these is to set out the priority areas for further work in preparing the associate for membership, and central to the monitoring of implementation will be the institutions of each association (EC Commission 1997a: IV.2). However, it is not the association council that determines the content of and amendments to the accession partnership, but the Commission and the Council of Ministers in partnership with the applicant state. Moreover, part of the reinforced accession strategy is participation in EC programmes and machinery for applying the *acquis*. These too are separate from the association.

Beyond the reinforced accession strategy, there are other elements of the accession process in which associations do not play a central role. First, there is the multilateral European conference which replaces the structured dialogue. Secondly, there is extra aid and financial assistance made available to CEE applicants. This is coordinated either within the accession partnership or by PHARE. Finally, there is the annual review of each applicant's preparedness for accession negotiations. Although this is based in part on presentations at meetings held under the auspices of the Europe Agreement, it is a report compiled by the Commission into which the association institutions themselves have no direct input. That said, in its first annual report on progress being made by states involved in the accession process, the Commission did seek to focus attention back on the institutions of association established by Europe Agreements noting that these 'continue to be the *privileged framework* within which the adoption of the acquis communautaire is regularly examined' (EC Commission 1998b: VII.4, emphasis added).

implemented 'significant elements'. Hungary, meanwhile, had 'met the bulk of its obligations' and Slovenia, although its Europe Agreement had yet to come into force, was deemed to have made 'some progress' in applying the corresponding dispositions of the Interim Agreement. Slovakia was reported as having 'for the most part met its obligations...and mostly according to the timetable for implementation'.

This has since been emphasized in the minutes of association council meetings. These refer to the association council 'fulfilling its central role in EU-[associate] relations'.[24] What this means in reality will only become known as the accession process evolves.

It is, however, clear that although the strategic objective of the Europe Agreements has been reoriented to membership, association is only one of several mechanisms to be used. The same is true for Cyprus and will be, once it is allowed back on board the process, for Malta. Arguably, this is to be welcomed. The contribution of earlier associations to the achievement of accession has been limited and suggests that association alone is an insufficient mechanism on its own to act as a stepping-stone to membership.

Association as a Stepping-Stone to Membership

For the CEE countries, the shift in purpose of the Europe Agreements has obviously been welcomed. With the Europe Agreements being reoriented as part of pre-accession and accession processes, the associations can clearly be viewed as a stepping-stone to EU membership. The same is arguably true of the associations with Cyprus and Malta. This does not mean to say that the associations actually constitute stepping-stones that can guarantee membership. In the cases of Greece and Turkey, the contribution of earlier associations to the realization of membership ambitions was and has been limited. They may have been perceived as stepping-stones to membership, but this does not mean that they actually lead to membership. Similarly, in other instances, association has proved a useful antechamber or waiting room for membership. Yet simply being in an antechamber does not guarantee entry through the next door into the EC/EU. The door has to be opened from inside.

The fact that Greece joined the EC in 1981 suggests that the association was a success in preparing Greece for membership, particularly since the Athens Agreement envisaged 1984 as the earliest date for accession. There can be little doubt, however, that the contribution of association to facilitating entry into the EC was considerably less than might have been anticipated. Indeed, accession has arguably occurred

24. See, for example, *Fifth Meeting of the Association Council between the European Union and Hungary—Joint Press Release*, UE-H 1513/98, 10 November 1998, point 1.

in spite of rather than because of association, an argument reinforced by the fact that Greece did not even mention the references to accession in the preamble to and Article 72 of the Athens Agreement when applying. Furthermore, when considering the long transitional period required by Greece to adopt the *acquis communautaire* and the subsequent, and indeed persistent, difficulties the country has had in adapting to EC norms and procedures—whether as a result of limited economic development or lack of political maturity—the value of the association appears to have been extremely limited. However, officials involved in Greece's accession negotiations do argue that the association was useful in bringing Greece closer to the EC in those areas where it did function (e.g. trade liberalization) (Nielsen 1979: 13-15, Tsalicoglou 1995: 141-42).[25] It is also argued that the internal organizational structure developed by Greece to deal with association was successfully adapted once the country joined the EC (Tsalicoglou 1995: 47). Even so, the absence of progress in other areas of envisaged activity (e.g. CAP harmonization, competition policy, free movement of services and capital, the CET), meant that the association's contribution was limited. Moreover, EC policies had evolved since 1961 without any accompanying evolution of the association.

The limited value of association in relationship to the attainment of membership is also evident in the case of Turkey, the EC's oldest associate. Despite having concluded an association agreement in 1963 and despite the agreement being designed to facilitate Turkish accession to the EEC at a later date, Turkey is arguably at the end of the current queue for EU membership. There are various reasons for this, not least the presence of various CEE countries which are deemed to be economically and politically more eligible for membership. The key points to be made here are that association has neither led to membership, nor conferred on Turkey any privileged status in terms of accession. Indeed, the association has been regarded on the Turkish side as essentially a failure in terms of preparing the country for membership. Without doubt, the poor functioning, unsatisfactory development and near breakdown of the association on several occasions were key factors in the decision of the Turkish government to apply for EC membership in April 1987. It was certainly felt at the time that the association had dated badly and no longer suited Turkish needs. Only

25. Nielsen was Director of the Commission's Delegation to the negotiations, while Tsalicoglu was a member of the Greek negotiating team.

membership could overcome the key problems with the association: persistent Greek obstructionism; limited preferential access to the EC markets for Turkish exports of textiles and clothes imports; the failure to provide for the free movement of workers; and access to financial assistance.

The EC's response to the application recognized implicitly that the association had so far failed to deliver. The Commission opinion issued on 18 December 1989 and endorsed by the Council in February 1990 argued against Turkish membership in the short and medium term (EC Commission 1989). Instead, it proposed exploiting the association to the full by concentrating on completing the customs union envisaged in the Ankara Agreement, resuming and intensifying financial cooperation, promoting industrial and technical cooperation, and strengthening political and cultural links. A similar set of proposals on future relations was issued six months later by the Commission (EC Commission 1990c). This proposed little more than a revitalization of the association. Later, in 'Europe and the Challenge of Enlargement', the Commission proposed that the association agreement should be 'more actively and effectively applied', and that the EC 'should take all appropriate steps to anchor [Turkey] firmly within the future architecture of Europe' (EC Commission 1992: 29). This was supposed to be achieved with the signing of the customs union agreements in 1995. The customs union agreement was also meant to keep Turkey on course for EU membership. Hence, it makes reference to Article 28 of the Ankara Agreement. Turkey's eligibility for membership has since been reiterated both in meetings of the Association Council and at European Council summits. Whether this means that Turkey will gain membership is obviously open to question. Based on the experience of association to date, they are few grounds for optimism.

Although neither conceived as a stepping-stone nor reoriented at any point to membership, the EEA provides the most obvious example to date of an association which has actually resulted in accessions to the EU. Out of the six EFTA participants, Austria, Finland, Norway and Sweden all successfully negotiated membership in 1993–94. Had the Norwegian people not rejected accession in a referendum, all four would have joined the EU on 1 January 1995. As it was, only Austria, Finland and Sweden participated in the fifth enlargement. Since this was only one year after the EEA entered into force, the contribution of the association was arguably limited in providing a stepping-stone to membership. That said, as a waiting room for states intent on membership, the EEA did provide the EFTA states with opportunities to prepare themselves for accession. Indeed, as early as 1992, Commission officials were referring to the EEA as a 'European waiting room, an ante-chamber' (Krenzler 1992: 71). The European Council, too, viewed the EEA as an interim measure. In June 1992 at Lisbon, it announced that membership negotiations with EFTA applicants would begin immediately after the Maastricht Treaty had been ratified.

With accession negotiations starting in February (Austria, Finland and Sweden) and April (Norway) 1993, the EEA became little more than a transitional regime. It did, however, contribute to applicants' preparations for membership by adjusting domestic administrative structures and policy processes to facilitate compliance with EC norms after the EEA Agreement entered into force. Successful completion of the EEA negotiations also meant that approximately 70% of accession negotiations had already been covered. Even when such a high figure is implicitly questioned, it is recognized that the conclusion of the EEA Agreement made a significant contribution to the relatively swift completion of the accession negotiations. The experiences of association per se, however, are undeniably limited. By the time accession negotiations had been completed in April 1994, the association created by the EEA Agreement was less than four months old.

Summary

Experiences of association have clearly been mixed. Obviously, it is too early to draw any firm conclusions regarding those associations created in the 1990s. Few are more than five years old. Moreover, the existence of pre-accession strategies, multilateral dialogue and accession partnerships mean that identifying clearly what role association plays in the development of CEE states relations with the EC/EU is no easy task. For long-standing associations conclusions can be more easily drawn. Generally, experiences of association have fallen short of expectations and provided a less than harmonious basis for relations. Indeed, Redmond goes so far as to say that the older association agreements have generally failed (1997: 8). Certainly, none of the early associations with Greece, Turkey, Cyprus or Malta provides an example of a dynamic and particularly beneficial relationship with the EC. Experiences of long-standing associations reflect more a sense of frustration on the part of the associate and indeed on the part of the EC. Freezings and crises have been all too frequent. In some cases, the relationship has scarcely existed. Trade has expanded, but has been accompanied by an increasing deficit with the EC. Cooperation has been limited. And institutional contacts have often been tense. Added to this, there is little evidence to suggest that association has played anything more than a marginal role in helping associates achieve the goal of membership. Trade benefits appear to accrue more to the EC. Aid has been limited.

The record of more recently established associations suggests more satisfactory relationships. Most associations appear to function smoothly. None has experienced crisis and most associates find themselves involved in pre-accession arrangements. This is not to say that concerns have not been voiced about association. Tariffs and quotas on trade between the EC and CEE associates could have been removed more quickly. Financial assistance could have been greater. And given that associates are increasingly expected to align their own legislation with that of the EC, more of a say in decision-making would be welcomed by many associates. Bilateral meetings generally could take place more frequently, and political dialogue should have been more of an exchange of ideas and concerns rather than the EC monologue that seems to have characterized many meetings.

Despite concerns about the realities of the relationship, association has clearly enjoyed a revival since the late 1980s. For the EC/EU it has proved to be a useful mechanism for meeting some of the aims of its neighbours while ensuring that it can continue with its own integration. Association now provides the basis for the EC/EU's relations with the majority of European states. Clearly, lessons about association can be drawn from these states' experiences. Lessons too can be drawn from the fact that there is barely a handful of associates willing to view their association as anything other than an interim arrangement before accession to the EU. Almost every associate currently seeks entry into the EU. Yet with the EU enlarging only slowly and not all aspirant states in a position to join, the lessons which can be drawn from the different forms of association and the various experiences of associates to date could well inform relations between the EU and a significant number of states for years to come.

4 |

Lessons of Association

The purpose of this final chapter is to draw together some of the lessons that can be gained from the types of association created and the experiences of those associates. As with the first chapter, the opening section focuses on the flexibility of association. It does, however, draw attention to the constraints on this flexibility, noting the central role played by the self-interest of the EC/EU. The second section examines association as an alternative to membership. Although viewed as such by several states, the significant shortcomings of association and the fact that it bestows on the associate the position of de facto satellite severely limits its attractiveness. Hence, as the third section notes, many associations are simply viewed, at least by the associate, as a stepping-stone to membership. Yet, to perceive association as such is to ignore the realities of both association and the EU enlargement process. Never has association led automatically to membership. Moreover, the contribution which association makes is arguably limited. The key determinant in whether an eligible state accedes to the EU is whether the EU wishes and is able to admit it. Association should not therefore be viewed as a stepping-stone to membership. In the light of this, the fourth section provides an assessment of the prospects for existing associations. With some states unlikely to accede to the EU in the foreseeable future, association will remain the basis for relations. The fifth section assesses the prospects for further associations being established with European states. A final section consists of some concluding remarks on association.

Association as a Flexible Form of Relationship with the EC

As argued in Chapter 2, the variety of associations that have been created attest the flexibility of association. Different agreements envisage different trade regimes, although all of them are based on at least free trade in industrial goods. Levels of cooperation vary and the extent of the commitments differ. Associations do, however, have common features. Institutional frameworks tend to have the same basic structure. Moreover, there has been an increasing tendency to require associates to approximate or harmonize their domestic legislation with that of the EC. All the same, the extent of this process differs from one association to another, thus emphasizing the fact that there is no one form of association.

The flexibility is not restricted to the forms of association that can be created. It also extends to the purpose of the relationship. Here, there is no common strategic goal. Few associations have been explicitly designed to lead to EC/EU membership. This is despite early attempts to view association as a stepping-stone to that end. The flexibility of association can also be seen in the fact that the strategic goal of the relationship can change. The establishment of an explicit link at Copenhagen in June 1993 between association via the Europe Agreements and EU membership is one clear example. This is not to say that associations always become pre-accession relationships. Indeed, in the case of Turkey, the opposite is true. Originally regarded as a staging post to membership, perceptions of the association have changed. Certainly from the point of view of the EC/EU, the association is increasingly regarded as a sui generis arrangement and a semi-permanent basis for relations. In this case, the flexibility of association has also meant ambiguity.

The ambiguity and flexibility of association have generally been welcomed. This has been reflected in the EC's reluctance to define exactly what association involves. For would-be associates the flexibility of association is also welcome. Associations can be tailored to their needs and aspirations. There is, however, one significant drawback. Association is an instrument of the EC's external relations. Hence, it is the EC which determines the content. This can be clearly seen in the EU's refusal to include any commitment to future membership in the Europe Agreements despite the fact that this was eagerly sought by the CEE states. Similarly, the protectionist attitude towards the granting of trade concessions in sensitive areas throughout the history of association emphasizes the dominant role played by the EC in the negotiation of agreements.

The preponderance of the EC/EU position is also reflected in the development of associations. Admittedly, where there is a wish to downgrade relations, as in the case of Mintoff's Malta in the 1970s, the associate can determine the status of the association. If, however, the wish of the associate is to see the association develop or be upgraded, then all will depend on the EC. The EC–Cyprus association, for example, failed to develop beyond the first stage until the second half of the 1980s, owing to the EC. The centrality of the EC's political will and perceptions of its own self-interest were evident when the European Economic Area (EEA) was proposed. Here, the Commission in particular was proactive in promoting association in an attempt to defer, if not deter, membership applications so that the energies of the EC could remain focused on its own integration and not be redirected towards enlargement. Self-interest also determined the way in which the EC devised and negotiated the first Europe Agreements in 1990–91. As Kennedy and Webb observe, the EC clearly did not wish to upset its internal development. Its response reflected '*its* timetable for integration, *its* trade needs, *its* perceived financial limits and absorptive capacity, in short *its* model of the possible' (1993: 1097). The content and purpose of association reflects more the interests and needs of the EC/EU.

Association as an Alternative to Membership

The centrality of the EC's position affects not only negotiations but also the reality of association. The relationship therefore is clearly unbalanced. This tends to lead to, or strengthen, membership aspirations. Hence, most associates regard association as an interim relationship that will help them accede to the EC/EU. There are, however, some states that see it as an alternative, at least in the short to medium term, to membership. Currently there are only three associates which share such a view, these being the three EFTA states participating in the EEA: Iceland, Liechtenstein and Norway.

Each appears quite satisfied with association as an alternative to membership. In 1995, the Foreign Minister of Iceland, Jón Baldvin Hannibalsson, stated that the EEA would 'continue to serve as the bedrock for relations between Iceland and the European Union', adding that 'it is quite clear that the EEA Agreement offers great possibilities for extended cooperation with our trading partners and allies in Europe, which should be fostered to their greatest extent in the interests of

Iceland'.[1] Moreover, Icelandic governments view membership as
unattractive on account of the existence of the Common Fisheries
Policy. Thus, there is a keenness to see the EEA develop further.

Liechtenstein too appears content with the EEA. Not only does it
provide access to the EU market which, along with EFTA, accounts for
approximately 60% of its exports, but to date at least, taxes, bank confi-
dentiality and the peculiarities of the principality's liberal company law
have remained untouched. Added to this, there is a feeling that it is
easier for Liechtenstein to obtain special treatment regarding sensitive
issues as a non-member than it is for full members of the EU (Gstöhl
1997: 171). As for EU membership, this is not viewed as a viable
policy option. The administrative burdens (e.g. providing officials and
holding the Council Presidency) would be too great for a state less than
one-tenth the size of Luxembourg.

For Norway, the EEA appears to provide an acceptable basis for
relations with the EU. Access to the internal market is effectively guaranteed and there is participation in numerous EC programmes. Added
to this, there is some access to decision shaping. Experiences to date
suggest that the existence of several Nordic states within the EU does
enable Norwegian interests in particularly sensitive areas to be noted
(e.g. gas liberalization, fisheries). Moreover, participation in the EEA
allows governments in Norway to avoid another divisive domestic
debate over membership. At least for the present, the EEA represents a
politically acceptable halfway house between membership and exclusion.

Despite such arguments in favour of the EEA, there is no guarantee
that it will always be viewed as a suitable alternative to membership.
As with other associations, it has several shortcomings which make it
unattractive to associates. These have a tendency to undermine its
attraction as a permanent alternative to membership. The first concerns
the commitments involved in an association. Here the key issue is that
association is essentially an unbalanced relationship in which the associate is required to adapt to EC norms and adopt EC rules. The EC does
not adapt to the associate. For example, almost universally, associates
are required to adopt EC norms concerning competition, and to
approximate national laws to EC legislation. In addition, the EEA
involves adoption of EC legislation, the Cypriot and Turkish customs

---

1. *Foreign Minister's Address to the Althingi*, Ministry for Foreign Affairs,
Reykjavik, 9 February 1995.

union obliges these states to adopt the Common Commercial Policy (CCP), and finally, the provisions of Greece's former association agreement committed it to policy harmonization. Such requirements place associates in the position of de facto satellite to the EC.

Secondly, there is the requirement that associates interpret EC legislation in the light of rulings from the ECJ. This is most explicit in the case of the EEA where there is the commitment to maintain homogeneity. Early studies of EFTA Court rulings suggest that they are based almost exclusively on EC case law and the reasoning of the ECJ (Kroenenberger 1996). It is noticeable too that the legal framework of the EEA has led to changes in legal reasoning and in some legal principles in Norway (Sverdrup 1998: 155). Adherence to ECJ rulings is not, however, confined to the EEA. The EC–Turkey customs union agreement of 1995 also requires interpretations of provisions corresponding to those in the Treaty of Rome 'in conformity with' the relevant decisions of the ECJ. All this emphasizes the unbalanced nature of association and the de facto satellization it entails.

This is also true of decision-making within associations. Associates have no say in EC decision-making even though they often have to abide by the outcomes. In the case of Greece's association, the institutional framework provided no real input into decisions of the EC. Where policy harmonization was required, this involved Greek alignment to existing and future EC policy. The same is true of the EEA. Despite decision-shaping, adherence to the principle of EC decision-making autonomy is strict. No EFTA state has either the opportunity or the power to veto the adoption of new legislation by the EC relating to the EEA. Hence, as Weiss argues:

> the whole extraordinary complex and scarcely transparent procedure is little more than 'collective and reactive' *ex-post facto* implementation of EC law…no more than a process for achieving consensus about taking over EC law *tel-quel* in the EEA area (1992: 421-22).

Others view the EEA in a similar light. As Schwok notes:

> Brussels has imposed its solution, leading to a '*de facto*' satellization of the EFTA states by forcing them to lose more independence if they stay outside the Community than if they join it (1992: 67).

In effect, EFTA states participating in the EEA lose more sovereignty by the absence of decision-making than they would by becoming members of the EU. The same applies to other associations even where homogeneity is not a requirement. Associates are obliged to abide by EC norms and rules in an increasing number of areas despite the fact that they have no input into EC decision-making. It should therefore come as no surprise that several associates have cited the decision-making shortcomings of association as one of the main reasons for applying for membership. A growing awareness on the part of Nordic states that the EEA would not involve decision-making certainly contributed to their membership applications. The same is true in the case of Malta. For example, an official report for the government in 1990 argued:

> further integration without participation of Malta's politicians in decision-making and structuring would be for Malta no real solution. It would force Malta to follow others and this would invariably, though possibly inadvertently, lead to discrimination at Malta's expense (Maltese EC Directorate 1990: 366-67).[2]

For associates, the absence of a decision-making role is arguably the fundamental shortcoming of association. As far as the EC is concerned, its decision-making autonomy is non-negotiable. Associates cannot be granted any direct involvement in decision-making. The implication of this is clear: association involves de facto satellization.

This raises the question of which states can accept association as an alternative to membership. In the past, reference was often made to those states (i.e. the neutrals) which, owing to their international commitments, could not accede to a supranational organization. With the end of the Cold War and the apparent redundancy of neutrality, this argument is no longer relevant. There are, however, three types of states which today could view association as an acceptable alternative to membership. The first is the very small yet economically rich state which would find the administrative burdens of membership too great. The obvious example here is Liechtenstein. Secondly, association as an alternative to membership is attractive to states where the issues of sovereignty and national independence enjoy high levels of political resonance and the debate over the fundamental flaws of association is under-developed. Norway is a case in point.[3] The third type of state is

2.   Earlier, the report had argued that membership 'would offer more opportunities to influence developments, more options and more freedom of action' (Maltese EC Directorate 1990: 363).

3.   An earlier example is Austria. In the 1960s, Austrian governments consciously avoided using the term 'association' to describe its envisaged relationship

one which finds itself unable to accede to the EU owing to fundamental difficulties it would have in adapting to one or more EC or EU policies. Iceland, for instance, is unwilling to contemplate EU membership given that it would have to abide by the Common Fisheries Policy. For all other states, association can only be regarded as a transitional step towards membership. Rarely can it offer a middle way between marginalization from the European integration process and membership of the EU.

Moving away from issues of decision-making and the resultant de facto satellization, a fourth shortcoming of association reflects the limited benefits which accrue from such a relationship, particularly when they are compared with what can be obtained via membership. First, there is the question of access to EC markets, notably for sensitive goods. As associates, states rarely enjoy free access, particularly for agricultural products. By contrast, membership would provide not only full access, but also participation in the CAP. For many states where the agricultural sector enjoys only limited financial support domestically the attractions of the Common Agricultural Policy are obvious. Secondly, associates receive only limited financial assistance from the EC to help them in their economic and social development. Admittedly, when the first association agreements were signed, the EC's involvement in regional development and social policy was limited. Since the 1970s, however, the increased attention being paid to the promotion of economic and social cohesion within the EC has meant that vast sums have become available through the structural funds. For associates, most of which are less economically developed than the majority of EU Member States, a major attraction of membership is access to such assistance. Finally, as the EC has established more associations, the privileged status implied by association has been undermined. There are today, for example, 16 European associates. In addition, there are the various associations which the EC has previously concluded and continues to upgrade with extra-European states in the Mediterranean which are often the economic competitors of European associates. The privileged status has also been undermined by the development of various partnership arrangements with the likes of the United States and Russia.

with the EC given the implied loss of independence and sovereignty. The preferred descriptions included 'agreement of a special nature' and '*sui generis* treaty'.

So, although there are states that view association as an alternative to EU membership, the shortcomings of associate status are such that the relationship holds few attractions for most. Not surprisingly therefore, the overwhelming majority have sought at some point to move beyond association and accede to the EC/EU. This raises the question of what contribution association makes to the attainment of membership. Here, much will depend on the position of the EC/EU. Clearly though, the EC/EU finds association in itself attractive. Having such a flexible mechanism available and being in a position to determine the content of any association means that the EC/EU can construct arrangements which generate benefits and are suited to its own needs and priorities. Association results in greater market access for EU producers and can involve wide-ranging cooperation. The EC/EU can also use association to accommodate many of the integration aspirations of non-Member States without having to undergo enlargement. A sense of belonging, and by implication security, can be exported. The EC/EU can also promote reform through the conditionality attached to the establishment and functioning of associations. Moreover, where the accession of a state is envisaged, association can be used to promote integration while the EC/EU concentrates on its own development and preparations for enlargement.

Association and EU Enlargement

Analyses of different associations have concluded that association entails preparation for membership. Thus, according to Kramer (1988: 163), association has the advantage of allowing a state to adapt to the EC's legal mechanisms to such an extent that membership should not pose too many or any large problems. Lycourgos (1994: 318-26) goes further and argues that the purpose of association is to make accession to the EC possible for those countries unable to become Member States immediately. Yet there is little evidence to suggest that any association so far has been successful in achieving this. As argued in Chapter 3, experiences of association show that the relationship has more often than not fallen short of expectations.

Indeed, membership applications have often been submitted due to the failure of the association to deliver satisfactory results. Member-ship—complete with full participation in EC policies, access to structural funds, and participation in decision-making—had become a far more attractive and desirable alternative to association. That said, only four states with experience of association have actually acceded to the EC/EU to date: Greece joined the EC in 1981; Austria, Finland and Sweden joined the EU in 1995. The contribution that each association made is open to question. The case of Greece has already been discussed (see pp. 110-11). As for the three former EFTA states, the experience of association was very brief, lasting only one year. Moreover, the shortcomings of decision-making were less pronounced given that for much of 1994 the three states had access to all Commission committees and observer status at Council working groups.

Other associates intent on membership have had to remain content with their associations in anticipation of accession at a later, unspecified date. Never has the EC/EU committed itself to admitting an associate on or by a given date. The strategic goals of applicant states' associations have, however, undergone a reorientation with accession now being acknowledged as the desired outcome. Seemingly, where accession is desired by an associate, the association is being portrayed as a stepping-stone to membership. Question marks must be raised, however, over whether any given association will actually lead to membership. Turkey is a case in point. Here, association has not served as a stepping-stone to membership. Turkey signed its association agreement in 1963 and of the states currently seeking EU membership it has had its application on the table longest. Despite being of far greater importance to the EU in trade terms than any CEE associate except Poland and despite its geostrategic position, Turkey is the associate which is furthest away from obtaining EU membership. Admittedly, the domestic political and economic situation in the country has not always enhanced Turkey's membership prospects. Yet, the association itself has hardly served in any substantive way as a stepping-stone to membership. Even if the customs union does function effectively, there is no guarantee at all that accession will follow.

Other associates currently find themselves in a more favourable position. Since the mid-1990s, their associations have become part of strategies designed ostensibly to prepare individual associates for accession. The proof of whether these will be successful will be the actual accession of current associates to the EU. If the six associates (Cyprus, the Czech Republic, Estonia, Hungary, Poland and Slovenia) which began negotiating accession in 1998 accede to the EU, association could be viewed as a successful stepping-stone to membership.

Other associates will take heart. Yet, there are several points which should be borne in mind concerning the contribution that association may be making to the membership prospects of current associates. These tend to suggest that the role of association is marginal and that the membership prospects of individual associates have more to do with the self-interest of the EU.

A first point concerns the contribution that association is playing in preparing applicant states for membership. As noted in the previous chapter, individual associations are only one element in the pre-accession strategies developed for each associate. Initially, they were accompanied by the 1995 White Paper and structured dialogue. They now find themselves sitting alongside accession partnerships, the European Conference, and pre-accession aid. The fact that the EU has introduced these new mechanisms clearly suggests that it regards association agreements by themselves as inadequate mechanisms for preparing applicants for membership. Moreover, applicant states do not hide their scepticism towards association. The failure of association to deliver Turkish accession to the EU demonstrates to any applicant state that association on its own is not necessarily a stepping-stone to membership.

A second point concerns the actual contribution that association makes towards a state meeting the economic criteria for membership. As the European Council declared at Copenhagen, no state may accede to the EU unless it possesses a functioning market economy as well as the capacity to cope with the competitive pressures and market forces which exist within the EU economy. This has been a major challenge for CEE associates given the systemic and structural changes they have had to undergo since 1989. Yet, whether association actually either facilitates or assists these changes and the development of functioning market economies can be questioned. Certainly, the EC can be criticized for not providing sufficient financial assistance to the CEE states. Equally, restricted access to EC markets for sensitive goods and in particular agricultural exports did not help reduce the pain of transition. Moreover, it is questionable whether the voluntary harmonization provisions of association agreements and the 1995 White Paper actually serve the interests of the CEE states. Evans (1997) argues that they may undermine the economic development of CEE associates. It may enhance in legal terms the extent to which an applicant meets the criteria for membership, but the process rarely takes into account the structural economic problems that the state is facing. A similar argument can be advanced with regard to the demands of association relating to competition policy.

The third point to be made concerns the process of enlargement generally. Irrespective of whether the strategic objective of an association is or becomes EU membership, no state can be guaranteed admittance to the EU. States will only gain entry if the EU agrees to admit them. This depends on various factors, not least whether the EU wishes and is able to expand its membership, but also whether the existing Member States unanimously agree to enlarge. Not to be forgotten is the European Parliament. It must give its assent to any enlargement. The implication of this is clear: to view association as a stepping-stone to membership is misleading. Use of a stepping-stone implies not only assistance in maintaining the momentum towards a given goal but also the achievement of that goal. The nature of EU enlargement cannot guarantee that the goal is achieved. This is of particular relevance for future enlargements of the EU.

Indeed, although an accession process has been launched, only six states actually began formal negotiations on membership in 1998. These negotiations are likely to lead to at least some if not all the affected states acceding to the EU. With so much attention focused on enlargement and so many statements being issued to the effect that it is the wish of the EU to enlarge, it is politically impossible for the EU not to admit new members. Hence, within the next five years or so, Cyprus, the Czech Republic, Estonia, Hungary, Poland and Slovenia could well become members of the EU. Yet, simply because the EU has launched an accession process does not mean that all the states involved will join. Significant issues will have to be addressed if the EU is to enlarge further. An inability or unwillingness to introduce institutional and policy reform beyond that envisaged in *Agenda 2000* could deny applicant states the membership that they so eagerly seek. Similarly, experiences of admitting one group of CEE states could deter the EU from admitting more. Hence, for the likes of Bulgaria, Latvia, Lithuania, Romania and Slovakia, association could remain a permanent basis for relations. The EU's own position on enlargement in the future could permanently undermine the notion that association is some form of stepping-stone to membership.

The Prospects for Existing Associations

For the vast majority of associates, membership is the main objective of their existing relationship with the EU. The future of their association will therefore depend heavily on the progress that is made towards accession. However, the link between association and membership is very much determined by the EU's approach towards enlargement and its views on the suitability of an applicant state to be admitted. This is no more apparent than in the case of Turkey. Notwithstanding the fact that the association is supposed to promote Turkish accession to the EU, Turkish membership of the EU attracts little support among EU Member States. Successive Greek governments have shown little if any desire to see Turkey accede to the EU. The same can also be said for the governments of other Member States, although they have had a tendency to be less public about their opposition and let the blame for tensions in EU–Turkey relations be placed on Greece. Although there are good grounds not to extend membership to Turkey immediately, it is such political opposition on the part of Member States that mainly explains the non-inclusion of Turkey in the accession process when launched by the EU in March 1998. There is little reason to expect a reversal in the EU position. So, for Turkey, association would appear to be the most likely basis for relations for the foreseeable future.

This is certainly the underlying message of the various measures which have been adopted in EU–Turkey relations since the mid-1990s. Admittedly, the preamble to the 1995 customs union agreement did note Turkey's membership aspirations through a reference to Article 28 of the Ankara Agreement. Yet, for the EU at least, the purpose of the customs union was to rejuvenate the association as the basis for long-term relations. Moreover, although Turkey's eligibility for EU membership was subsequently reaffirmed in the Commission's progress report published in November 1998, the publication of *Agenda 2000* 18 months earlier contained only limited reference to Turkey leaving proposals for the development of relations to a separate communication. The implication was that Turkey was not being included in the EU's plans for enlargement. As for the Commission's proposals, these centred around building on the foundations of the association agreement and the customs union (EC Commission 1997c). Since then, in an attempt to reassure its longest-standing associate of its European vocation, the EU has developed a 'European Strategy' for Turkey.

Ostensibly, this is designed to prepare the country for membership. In essence, however, its focus is deepening the customs union (EC Commission 1998c). Moreover, Turkey remains outside the accession process involving the CEE states and Cyprus and has not been granted an accession partnership.

Whether Turkey's commitment to the customs union and its association with the EC is sustained remains to be seen. Arguably, the customs union and existing proposals will create a very close relationship with the EC. Yet customs union requires an associate to assume many of the constraints of membership without being able to enjoy the benefits. In the case of Turkey, customs union involves taking on board EC decisions regarding the CCP without having a role in their formulations. This will undoubtedly restrict Turkey's ability to negotiate trade agreements with other states. As the Commission noted when reviewing regional cooperation efforts around the Black Sea, Turkey would not be in a position to participate in regional free trade agreements given its customs union with the EC (Akagül 1998: 366-67). Also, trade with Northern Cyprus will technically be banned.[4] Moreover, Turkey is required to adapt its legislation to that of EC in various areas concerning technical barriers to trade. The imbalance in the relationship is underlined by the fact that in those areas where Turkey might benefit, progress is neither immediate nor automatic. For example, the customs union does not involve free trade in agricultural goods from the outset. As for the free movement of labour, services and capital, this may be possible at a later date. Such a disequilibrium within the customs union could impact on the functioning of the association. Indeed, existing political disputes which have dominated relations in the 1990s could be intensified. Within Turkey, the sense of political discrimination could increase and strengthen anti-European forces. Instead of helping the EU and Turkey overcome their differences, the customs union could strain relations further (Kramer 1996: 71-72).

The association could also be undermined by the EU's enlargement process. This is important since the customs union was only accepted by Turkey because it was viewed as a step that launches in an irreversi-

---

4. In 1994, the ECJ issued a ruling that effectively bans trade between Northern Cyprus and the EU. Technically, customs union will require Turkey to abide by such a ruling. Whether it does, remains to be seen. So far, official Turkish policy is not to allow anything in the customs union to affect its relations with Northern Cyprus (Kramer 1996: 73).

ble manner the process of accession. First, if Cyprus does accede to the EU, then Greece could gain an ally in its opposition to Turkish accession. Turkey's chances of gaining membership will face an extra hurdle. Secondly, if the EU struggles to move beyond a first wave of eastward enlargement or gets distracted westwards, possibly to Switzerland and/or Norway, then any hopes of accession in the short to medium term will be further undermined. In such a situation where membership prospects fade, Turkey could well seek to loosen its ties with the EU. The question will surely be raised as to why Turkey should submit to the constraints of the customs union if membership is not going to result. Hence, it is possible that future experiences of association coupled with continued non-inclusion in the accession process could see a reversal in the integration efforts pursued on the basis of association. Association could result not in integration but estrangement (Kramer 1996: 73).

By contrast, Cyprus seems set for membership of the EU. This is despite reservations over admitting a divided island into the EU and the resultant alienation of Turkey. Cyprus began accession negotiations with the EU in 1998 and is arguably the best prepared of all candidates for membership. Added to this, Greece is threatening to veto the conclusion of accession treaties with CEE states if Cyprus is not included in the next enlargement. In such circumstances, the island's accession prospects are good. Yet a failure of negotiations cannot be totally ruled out. In such circumstances, the association would remain and provide the basis for relations. On balance, though, the days of the association look numbered.

The same cannot be said for Malta's association. Prior to 1996, Malta was in a similar position to Cyprus—marked for inclusion in the next round of EU enlargement. However, with the victory of the Labour Party in the 1996 election, the membership application was effectively frozen. Malta was therefore omitted from the accession process launched in 1998. The future of the association in the medium term at least seemed assured. Yet, as noted earlier, the reactivation of the 1990 membership application by the new Nationalist government in autumn 1998 was accompanied by strenuous efforts to get the EU to fast-track Malta and open accession negotiations. Some progress had been made in this direction at the time of writing. In February 1999 the Commission issued an update of its 1993 Opinion recommending that negotiations start at the end of the year (EC Commission 1999: C). If negotiations are opened and successfully concluded, then the association will soon become redundant. However, if, like some of the CEE associates (see below), Malta is not invited to participate in the forthcoming enlargement round, the association could be providing the basis for relations for some time to come. Indeed, pessimistic scenarios which argue that the EU may not enlarge beyond an initial wave suggest that it could become the permanent basis for relations.

For half the CEE applicants, the prospect of membership resulting from accession negotiations implies a limited future for their respective associations. They therefore find themselves in a position not dissimilar to Cyprus. For the other CEE states (Bulgaria, Latvia, Lithuania, Romania and Slovakia), the challenges which the EU faces in seeking to enlarge may delay membership for some time. Hence, association is likely to serve as a basis for relations for at least the medium term. An optimistic view of the enlargement process would predict, however, that some of these CEE states might be invited to open negotiations before an initial wave of enlargement has been completed. The Commission's favourable comments on Latvia in its 1998 progress report did suggest that this was possible (EC Commission 1998b: VII.2). Yet, less encouraging for these states is the limited enthusiasm which the EU currently has for enlargement. This makes it likely that there will be significant gap between a first round of enlargement and the next. This also raises the question of whether the EU will be able to expand beyond a membership of 20 or 21. These problems could result in associations providing a semi-permanent basis for relations. More-over, there may in the future be economic and political factors that lead the EU to refuse certain countries membership.

Indeed, in the case of those states which are weakest economically and lagging behind in the transition process (e.g. Romania), there is the possibility that the criteria for EU membership may never be met. In such cases, association could become permanent. Whether such a rela-tionship could be sustained given the shortcomings involved is open to question. Certainly, if the association is seen as having failed to provide the stepping-stone to membership envisaged, then enthusiasm for it will be limited. The commitment to economic and political reforms may falter too. A situation similar to that predicted above for the EC–Turkey association could develop. The sense that association had failed to deliver, particularly with regard to membership, would be underlined were the EU to turn its attention to other associates which are currently not formally part of the accession process. The fact that they may be pushed to the front of the queue of states awaiting entry to the EU cannot be ruled out. If they are, it may raise doubts again about the longevity of the EEA.

When in 1992 it became clear that most EFTA states were intent on EU membership and regarded the EEA as little more than an ante-chamber where they could wait for the enlargement process to be started, it seemed that the EEA would be short-lived. Norway's decision not to join the EU changed this, however, and the EEA survived intact. The fact that it appears to be functioning and developing to the general satisfaction of the participants would suggest that it will continue to provide the basis of relations between the EU, Iceland, Liechtenstein and Norway. With mechanisms for political dialogue being established and arrangements being made for involvement in Schengen-based arrangements, fears of total exclusion from matters covered by the CFSP and JHA pillars have been assuaged. That said, it is unlikely to attract new members. No CEE state has shown any enthusiasm for the EEA and no attempts have been made to require CEE states to join as part of their preparation for EU membership, as some have suggested (e.g. Peers 1995). Also, there would appear to be little likelihood of the Swiss government seeking to gain popular support for participation in the EEA. With a series of bilateral EC–Switzerland agreements concluded in 1998, relations have been upgraded and the EEA is no longer viewed as a worthwhile policy option. Moreover, sights appear to be firmly fixed on reactivating the 1992 membership application.

With no new members likely, the EEA's future could be placed in question if one of the three EFTA participants joined the EU. At present, none has a membership application pending although another Norwegian application cannot be ruled out. As the EEA agreement and its workings become better known to the public, the forces arguing in favour of EU membership (which oppose the EEA as a 'tenant contract' and for creating a 'fax democracy') and those opposing the EEA as entailing unprecedented adjustments will grow stronger (Bonde 1998). Whether the EEA would be able to survive such a debate is open to question. Certainly, if the Norwegian public did object to the EEA, support for EU membership could increase. If it did, and a future Norwegian government did apply to accede to the EU, Iceland may not be too far behind. The prospect of Norway joining the EU at the time of the 1995 enlargement certainly pushed the Icelandic government into considering an application for EU membership. It also raised doubts in the EU over whether an EEA involving only Iceland and Liechtenstein should be maintained.

Clearly, the future of existing associations is very much tied up with the dynamics of EU enlargement. Associates are generally keen to obtain membership and hardly any regard association as a desirable alternative to membership. Associations will, however, remain a central element of the EU's relations with various European states for the foreseeable future. Until associates are admitted to the EU, they will have to depend on their associations as a basis for relations. It is also possible that further associations will be created. As other CEE states become more stable and make further progress with democratization offers of association may be made.

The Prospects for Further Associations

For certain CEE states that are keen on strengthening their ties with the EU yet have not signed Europe Agreements with the EC, association is regarded as a desirable relationship. Governments in Albania, Moldova and Ukraine have all expressed a desire for association. Moreover, once the political situation stabilizes in the states of the former Yugoslavia, there is the possibility that new types of association may be developed to address the needs and aspirations of these states. Hence, association would appear to have a future.

However, the EC's hands are partially tied in how it uses association. Here, the declaration of the European Council at Copenhagen in June 1993 is of crucial importance. It stated that 'the associated countries of Central and Eastern Europe that so desire shall become members of the European Union'. Admittedly, any aspirant member must fulfil the various membership criteria before entry. But, the implication of the Copenhagen commitment is that any CEE state that signs an association agreement which enters into force is seemingly set for membership. Hence, unless the EU is willing to view a given state as a future member, then an association agreement is unlikely to be signed. Such a constraint on the use of association has already been seen. The Partnership and Cooperation Agreements with Russia, Ukraine and other former states of the USSR have been consciously concluded on the basis of Articles 113 (133) and 235 (308) of the Treaty of Rome. The

Council and Commission ruled out use of Article 238 (310) on the grounds that post-Copenhagen it was seen to create a relationship that would eventually lead to membership.

Such a decision does not mean to say that no further associations will be concluded. There are states that are undeniably situated within the European continent with which association is possible. Yet, to date there has generally been little enthusiasm either to conclude further Europe Agreements or to create new forms of association. Albania's 1992 trade and cooperation agreement with the EC does refer to 'the objective of an association agreement in due course' yet the Commission's 1995 assessment on the feasibility of an association with Albania concluded that a classical Europe Agreement could not be envisaged for economic reasons.

More recently, in the light of the crisis in Kosovo, the EU has become more receptive to Albanian aspirations. In April 1999, the Council gave its support to the Commission's urgent examination of an upgrading of contractual relations towards an association agreement. An identical statement was made with regard to the Former Yugoslav Republic of Macedonia.[5] Its 1997 Cooperation Agreement with the EC notes Macedonian aspirations for 'an advanced relationship towards an association'.[6] The aspiration was not openly supported by the EU. The situation in Kosovo may, however, reduce the likelihood of association being little more than a long-term possibility.

As for the Ukraine's request for a Europe Agreement, the reaction of the EU has been a polite yet firm 'no'. The preference is clearly for full implementation of the Partnership and Cooperation Agreement that entered into force in 1998.

Concluding Remarks

Few states that have experienced association would eagerly advocate the relationship as the ideal basis for relations with the EU. Its flexibility may mean that different associations can be created to accommodate the needs of different states. Yet there is a certain rigidity to the notion of association as it has been developed by the EC. Association requires adaptation to the EC. It requires the progressive integration of a state

5. *Council of the European Union Press Release*, 7561/99, Brussels, 26 April 1999: 9.

6. *OJ* L348, 18 December 1997, Article 45.

into the EC/EU system without the state concerned having any direct impact on the decisions and rules which govern this integration. Hence, association in its more developed forms is tantamount to de facto satellization. It is hardly surprising therefore that states have rejected it as an alternative to membership.

For other states, association is unattractive because it does not meet their desire to be a member of the EU. Hence, at best, association is seen as an interim arrangement which will lead to membership. It is misleading, however, to view association as some form of stepping-stone to membership of the EU. The automatic link does not exist. That said, few associates can afford to abandon association. It is the basis for the closest form of relationship possible with the EU and as such provides a useful training ground for membership. Via association, states can prove their eligibility for admission into the EU. Whether the association will be followed by membership though depends on the EU and the dynamics of enlargement. If the dynamics do not allow for states to be admitted, association will become not a stepping-stone but the alternative to membership.

Appendix 1

Association: Applications, Negotiations and Agreements

	Application submitted	Negotiations begin	Agreement Initialled	Agreement Signed	Agreement In force	OJ reference
Greece	08.06.1959	21.03.1960	30.03.1961	09.07.1961	01.11.1962	*JOCE* 26, 18.02.1963
Turkey	31.07.1959	10.04.1961	25.06.1963	12.09.1963	01.12.1964	*JOCE* 217, 29.12.1964
Austria	12.12.1961	19.03.1965	—	—	—	—
Sweden	12.12.1961	—	—	—	—	—
Switzerland	15.12.1961	—	—	—	—	—
Spain	09.02.1962	—	—	—	—	—
Portugal	18.05.1962	—	—	—	—	—
Malta	04.09.1967	07.04.1970	24.07.1970	05.12.1970	01.04.1971	*JOCE* L61, 14.03.1971
Cyprus	10.12.1962	24.01.1972	06.12.1972	19.12.1972	01.06.1973	*OJ* L133, 21.05.1973
EFTA States	—	20.06.1990	14.04.1992	02.05.1992	01.01.1994*	*OJ* L1, 03.01.1994
Hungary	—	21.12.1990	22.11.1991	16.12.1991	01.02.1994	*OJ* L347, 31.12.1993
Poland	—	22.12.1990	22.11.1991	16.12.1991	01.02.1994	*OJ* L348, 31.12.1993
Czechoslovakia	—	20.12.1990	22.11.1991	16.12.1991	—	—
Romania	—	19.05.1992	12.11.1992	01.02.1993	01.02.1995	*OJ* L357, 31.12.1994
Bulgaria	—	14.05.1992	22.12.1992	08.03.1993	01.02.1995	*OJ* L358, 31.12.1994
Czech Republic	—	15.04.1993	23.06.1993	04.10.1993	01.02.1995	*OJ* L360, 31.12.1994
Slovakia	—	15.04.1993	23.06.1993	04.10.1993	01.02.1995	*OJ* L359, 31.12.1994
Estonia	—	15.12.1994	12.04.1995	12.06.1995	01.02.1998	*OJ* L68, 09.03.1998
Latvia	—	15.12.1994	12.04.1995	12.06.1995	01.02.1998	*OJ* L26, 02.02.1998
Lithuania	—	15.12.1994	12.04.1995	12.06.1995	01.02.1998	*OJ* L51, 20.02.1998
Slovenia	—	15.03.1995	15.06.1995	10.06.1996	01.02.1999	*OJ* L51, 26.02.1999

* The EEA Agreement did not enter into force in Liechtenstein until 1 May 1995. The EEA Agreement did not enter into force in Switzerland.

Appendix 2

Association Agreements and
Membership Applications

	Association agreement		Membership
	Signed	Enters into force	application

States applying for membership once associates

Greece	09.07.1961	01.11.1962	12.06.1975
Turkey	12.09.1963	01.12.1964	14.04.1987
Malta	05.12.1970	01.04.1971	16.07.1990
Cyprus	19.12.1972	01.06.1973	04.07.1990
Hungary	16.12.1991	01.02.1994	31.03.1994
Poland	16.12.1991	01.02.1994	05.04.1994
Romania	01.02.1993	01.02.1995	22.06.1995
Bulgaria	08.03.1993	01.02.1995	14.12.1995
Czech Republic	04.10.1993	01.02.1995	17.01.1996
Slovakia	04.10.1993	01.02.1995	22.06.1995

States applying before association agreement enters into force

Switzerland	02.05.1992	failed to ratify	26.05.1992
Norway	02.05.1992*	01.01.1994	25.11.1992
Estonia	12.06.1995	01.02.1998	24.11.1995
Latvia	12.06.1995	01.02.1998	13.10.1995
Lithuania	12.06.1995	01.02.1998	08.12.1995

States applying on or before signing an association agreement

Austria	02.05.1992	01.01.1994	17.07.1989
Sweden	02.05.1992	01.01.1994	01.07.1991
Finland	02.05.1992	01.01.1994	18.03.1992
Slovenia**	10.06.1996	01.02.1999	10.06.1996

* Norway had already applied on two previous occasions (30.04.1962 and 21.07.1967).
** Slovenia applied immediately after the signing ceremony.

Appendix 3

Selected Treaty Provisions

The following Treaty Articles are those referred to in Chapter 1. The original wording of the provisions is contained in the left-hand column with subsequent changes being highlighted in *italics* under the relevant amending Treaty. The current wording appears in the right hand column.

Article 228 Originally	Single European Act	Maastricht Treaty	Article 300 Treaty of Amsterdam
1. Where this Treaty provides for the conclusion of agreements between the Community and one or more States or an international organisation, such agreements shall be negotiated by the Commission. Subject to the powers vested in the Commission in this field, such agreements shall be concluded by the Council after consulting the European Parliament where required by this Treaty The Council, the Commission or a Member State may obtain beforehand the opinion of the Court of Justice as to whether an agreement envisaged is compatible with the provisions of this Treaty. Where the opinion of the Court of Justice is adverse, the		*1. Where this Treaty provides for the conclusion of agreements between the Community and one or more States or international organisations, the Commission shall make recommendations to the Council, which shall authorise the Commission to open the necessary negotiations. The Commission shall conduct these negotiations in consultation with special committees appointed by the Council to assist it in this task and within the framework of such directives as the Council may issue to it.* *In exercising the powers conferred upon it by this paragraph, the Council shall act by a qualified majority, except in the cases provided for in the second sen-*	1. Where this Treaty provides for the conclusion of agreements between the Community and one or more States or international organisations, the Commission shall make recommendations to the Council, which shall authorise the Commission to open the necessary negotiations. The Commission shall conduct these negotiations in consultation with special committees appointed by the Council to assist it in this task and within the framework of such directives as the Council may issue to it. In exercising the powers conferred upon it by this paragraph, the Council shall act by a qualified majority, except in the cases *where the first subpara-*

Article 228 Originally	Single European Act	Maastricht Treaty	Article 300 Treaty of Amsterdam
agreement may enter into force only in accordance with Article 236. 2. Agreements concluded under these conditions shall be binding on the institutions of the Community and on Member States.	agreement may enter into force only in accordance with Article 236. 2. Agreements concluded under these conditions shall be binding on the institutions of the Community and on Member States.	tence of paragraph 2, for which it shall act unanimously. 2. Subject to the powers vested in the Commission in this field, the agreements shall be concluded by the Council, acting by a qualified majority on a proposal from the Commission. The Council shall act unanimously when the agreement covers a field for which unanimity is required for the adoption of internal rules, and for the agreements referred to in Article 238.	graph of paragraph 2 provides that the Council shall act unanimously. 2. Subject to the powers vested in the Commission in this field, the signing, which may be accompanied by a decision on provisional application before entry into force, and the conclusion of the agreements shall be decided on by the Council, acting by a qualified majority on a proposal from the Commission. The Council shall act unanimously when the agreement covers a field for which unanimity is required for the adoption of internal rules and for the agreements referred to in Article 310. By way of derogation from the rules laid down in paragraph 3, the same procedures shall apply for a decision to suspend the application of an agreement,

Article 228 Originally	Single European Act	Maastricht Treaty	Article 300 Treaty of Amsterdam
			and for the purpose of establishing the positions to be adopted on behalf of the Community in a body set up by an agreement based on Article 310, when that body is called upon to adopt decisions having legal effects, with the exception of decisions supplementing or amending the institutional framework of the agreement. The European Parliament shall be immediately and fully informed on any decision under this paragraph concerning the provisional application or the suspension of agreements, or the establishment of the Community position in a body set up by an agreement based on Article 310.
		3. The Council shall conclude agreements after consulting the European Parliament, except for the agreements referred to in	3. The Council shall conclude agreements after consulting the European Parliament, except for the agreements referred to in

Article 228 Originally	Single European Act	Maastricht Treaty	Article 300 Treaty of Amsterdam
		Article 113(3), including cases where the agreement covers a field for which the procedure referred to in Article 189b or that referred to in Article 189c is required for the adoption of internal rules. The European Parliament shall deliver its opinion within a time-limit which the Council may lay down according to the urgency of the matter. In the absence of an opinion within that time-limit, the Council may act.	Article 133(3), including cases where the agreement covers a field for which the procedure referred to in Article 251 or that referred to in Article 252 is required for the adoption of internal rules. The European Parliament shall deliver its opinion within a time-limit which the Council may lay down according to the urgency of the matter. In the absence of an opinion within that time-limit, the Council may act.
		By way of derogation from the previous subparagraph, agreements referred to in Article 238, other agreements establishing a specific institutional framework by organising cooperation procedures, agreements having important budgetary implications for the Community and agreements entailing amendment of an	By way of derogation from the previous subparagraph, agreements referred to in Article 310, other agreements establishing a specific institutional framework by organising cooperation procedures, agreements having important budgetary implications for the Community and agreements entailing amendment of an act

Article 228 Originally	Single European Act	Maastricht Treaty	Article 300 Treaty of Amsterdam
		act adopted under the procedure referred to in Article 189b shall be concluded after the assent of the European Parliament has been obtained.	adopted under the procedure referred to in Article 251 shall be concluded after the assent of the European Parliament has been obtained.
		The Council and the European Parliament may, in an urgent situation, agree upon a time-limit for the assent.	The Council and the European Parliament may, in an urgent situation, agree upon a time-limit for the assent.
		4. When concluding an agree-ment, the Council may, by way of derogation from paragraph 2, authorise the Commission to approve modifications on behalf of the Community where the agreement provides for them to be adopted by a simplified pro-cedure or by a body set up by the agreement; it may attach speci-fic conditions to such authorisa-tion.	4. When concluding an agree-ment, the Council may, by way of derogation from paragraph 2, authorise the Commission to approve modifications on behalf of the Community where the agreement provides for them to be adopted by a simplified pro-cedure or by a body set up by the agreement; it may attach specific conditions to such authorisation.
		5. When the Council envisages concluding an agreement which calls for amendments to the	5. When the Council envisages concluding an agreement which calls for amendments to this

Article 228 Originally	Single European Act	Maastricht Treaty	Article 300 Treaty of Amsterdam
		Treaty, the amendments must first be adopted in accordance with the procedure laid down in Article N of the Treaty on European Union	Treaty, the amendments must first be adopted in accordance with the procedure laid down in Article 48 of the Treaty on European Union.
		6. The Council, the Commission or a Member State may obtain the opinion of the Court of Justice as to whether an agreement envisaged is compatible with the provisions of this Treaty. Where the opinion of the Court of Justice is adverse, the agreement may enter into force only in accordance with Article N of the Treaty on European Union.	6. The Council, the Commission or a Member State may obtain the opinion of the Court of Justice as to whether an agreement envisaged is compatible with the provisions of this Treaty. Where the opinion of the Court of Justice is adverse, the agreement may enter into force only in accordance with Article 48 of the Treaty on European Union.
		7. Agreements concluded under the conditions set out in this Article shall be binding on the institutions of the Community and on Member States.	7. Agreements concluded under the conditions set out in this Article shall be binding on the institutions of the Community and on Member States.

Article 228a Originally	Single European Act	Maastricht Treaty	Article 301 Treaty of Amsterdam
		Where it is provided, in a common position or in a joint action adopted according to the provisions of the Treaty on European Union relating to the common foreign and security policy, for an action by the Community to interrupt or to reduce, in part or completely, economic relations with one or more third countries, the Council shall take the necessary urgent measures. The Council shall act by a qualified majority on a proposal from the Commission.	Where it is provided, in a common position or in a joint action adopted according to the provisions of the Treaty on European Union relating to the common foreign and security policy, for an action by the Community to interrupt or to reduce, in part or completely, economic relations with one or more third countries, the Council shall take the necessary urgent measures. The Council shall act by a qualified majority on a proposal from the Commission.

Article 237 Originally	Single European Act	Article O Maastricht Treaty	Article 48 Treaty of Amsterdam
Any European State may apply to become a member of the Community. It shall address its application to the Council, which shall act unanimously after obtaining the opinion of the Commission	Any European State may apply to become a member of the Community. It shall address its application to the Council, which shall act unanimously after consulting the Commission and after receiving the assent of the European Parliament which shall act by an absolute majority of its component members.	Any European State may apply to become a member of the Union. It shall address its application to the Council, which shall act unanimously after consulting the Commission and after receiving the assent of the European Parliament which shall act by an absolute majority of its component members.	Any European State *which resp- ects the principles set out in Article 6(1)* may apply to be- come a member of the Union. It shall address its application to the Council, which shall act unanimously after consulting the Commission and after receiving the assent of the European Parliament which shall act by an absolute majority of its component members.
	The conditions of admission and the adjustments to this Treaty necessitated thereby shall be the subject of an agreement between the Member States and the appli- cant State. This agreement shall be submitted for ratification by all the Contracting States in accordance with their respective constitutional requirements.	The conditions of admission and the adjustments to the Treaties on which the Union is founded which such admission entails shall be the subject of an agree- ment between the Member States and the applicant State. This agreement shall be submit- ted for ratification by all the Contracting States in accordance with their respective constitu- tional requirements.	The conditions of admission and the adjustments to the Treaties on which the Union is founded which such admission entails shall be the subject of an agree- ment between the Member States and the applicant State. This agreement shall be submit- ted for ratification by all the Contracting States in accordance with their respective constitu- tional requirements.
The conditions of admission and the adjustments to this Treaty necessitated thereby shall be the subject of an agreement between the Member States and the appli- cant State. This agreement shall be submitted for ratification by all the Contracting States in accordance with their respective constitutional requirements.			

Article 238 Originally	Single European Act	Maastricht Treaty	Article 310 Treaty of Amsterdam
The Community may conclude with a third State, a union of States or an international organization agreements establishing an association involving reciprocal rights and obligations, common action and special procedures.	The Community may conclude with a third State, a union of States or an international organization agreements establishing an association involving reciprocal rights and obligations, common action and special procedures.	The Community may conclude with *one or more States or international organizations* agreements establishing an association involving reciprocal rights and obligations, common action and special procedures.	The Community may conclude with one or more States or international organizations agreements establishing an association involving reciprocal rights and obligations, common action and special procedures.
These agreements shall be concluded by the Council acting unanimously and after consulting the Assembly	These agreements shall be concluded by the Council acting unanimously and after receiving the assent of the European Parliament which shall act by an absolute majority of its component members		
Where such agreements call for amendments to this Treaty, these amendments shall first be adopted in accordance with the procedure laid down in Article 236	Where such agreements call for amendments to this Treaty, these amendments shall first be adopted in accordance with the procedure laid down in Article 236		

Bibliography[*]

Primary Sources

Accord créant une association entre la Communauté économique européenne et la Turquie, *JOCE* 217, 29 décembre 1964.

Accord créant une association entre la Communauté économique européenne et Malte, *JOCE* L61, 14 mars 1971.

Accord créant une association entre la Communauté économique européenne et la Grèce, *JOCE* 26, 18 février 1963.

Agreement Establishing an Association between the European Economic Community and the Republic of Cyprus, *OJ* L133, 21 May 1973.

Agreement on the European Economic Area, *OJ* L1, 3 January 1994.

Birkelbach, W.

1962   'Report of the Political Committee on the Political and Institutional Aspects of Accession to or Association with the European Economic Community', *European Parliament Working Paper Document*, No. 122, 15 January.

Blaisse, P.A.

1963   'Report on Behalf of the Committee on External Trade on the Common Trade Policy of the EEC towards Third Countries and on the Applications by European Countries for Membership or Association', *European Parliament Working Paper*, No. 134, 26 January.

Dehousse, F.

1967   'Report Drawn up on Behalf of the Political Committee on the Communities' Relations with Non-Member Countries and International Organizations', *European Parliament Working Document*, No. 134, 8 May.

EC Commission

1967   *Opinion on the Applications for Membership Received from the United Kingdom, Ireland, Denmark and Norway*, Commission of the European Communities, Brussels.

1968   'Opinion...on Certain Problems Resulting from the Applications for Membership Received from the United Kingdom, Ireland, Denmark and Norway', *Bull. EC* 1.4, Supplement.

1971   'Opinion...on Relations between the Enlarged Community and those EFTA Member States (Including the Associated Finland) that Have Not Applied for Membership of the Community', *Bull. EC* 4.3, Supplement.

---

[*]A fuller bibliography of sources relating to association can be found in D. Phinnemore, 'The Politics of Association: The European Community and the Use of Article 238, 1958–1995' (PhD Thesis, University of Kent at Canterbury, 1997).

EC Commission *continued*

1989　　*Opinion on Turkey's Request for Accession to the Community,* SEC(89) 2290 final, Brussels, 18 December.

1990a　　*Association Agreements with the Countries of Central and Eastern Europe: A General Outline,* COM(90)398 final, Brussels, 27 August.

1990b　　*The Development of the Community's Relations with the Countries of Central and Eastern Europe,* SEC(90)196 final, Brussels, 1 February.

1990c　　*Communication sur les relations avec la Turquie et proposition de décision du Conseil relative à la conclusion du IVème Protocole Financier,* SEC(90)1017 final, Brussels, 14 June.

1992　　'Europe and the Challenge of Enlargement', *Bull. EC* 25, Supplement 3.

1993a　　*Commission Opinion on the Application by the Republic of Cyprus for Membership,* COM(93)313 final, Brussels, 30 June.

1993b　　*Commission Opinion on Malta's Application for Membership,* COM(93) 312 final, Brussels, 30 June.

1994a　　*The Europe Agreements and Beyond: A Strategy to Prepare the Countries of Central and Eastern Europe for Accession,* COM(94)320 final, Brussels, 13 July.

1994b　　*Follow up to Commission Communication on 'The Europe Agreements and Beyond: A Strategy to Prepare the Countries of Central and Eastern Europe for Accession',* COM(94)361 final, Brussels, 27 July.

1995　　*Preparation of the Associated Countries of Central and Eastern Europe for Integration into the Internal Market of the Union,* COM(95)163 final, Brussels, 3 May 1995.

1997a　　*Agenda 2000.* II. *Communication: Reinforcing the Pre-Accession Strategy* COM (97) 2000 final, Brussels, 15 July.

1997b　　'Agenda 2000', *Bull. EU,* Supplements 6-15/97.

1997c　　*Communication on the Further Development of Relations with Turkey,* COM(97)394 final, Brussels, 15 July.

1998a　　*Regular Report on Progress towards Accession: Cyprus,* COM (98) 710 final, Brussels, 17 December.

1998b　　*Reports on Progress towards Accession by each of the Candidate Countries: Composite Paper,* COM (98) 712 final, Brussels, 17 December.

1998c　　*EU–Turkey Relations: Strategy for Relations between Turkey and the European Union,* ip/98/208, Brussels, 4 March.

1999　　*Report Updating the Commission's Opinion on Malta's Application for Membership,* COM(99)69 final, Brussels, 17 February.

EEC Commission

1959　　*First Memorandum of the Commission of the European Community to the Council of Ministers of the Community (Pursuant to the Decision of 3 December 1958), Concerning the Problems Raised by the Establishment of a European Economic Association,* Brussels, 26 February.

1962　　*Association with Neutral Countries: Questions Arising from Statements by the Representatives of Austria, Sweden, and Switzerland,* Report I/3/ 06524/62, EEC Commission, Brussels, 19 October.

EFTA　　*Annual Reports* (Geneva/Brussels: EFTA).

Europe Agreement Establishing an Association between the European Communities and
          their Member States, of the one part, and Bulgaria, of the other part,
          OJ L358, 31 December 1994.
Europe Agreement Establishing an Association between the European Communities and
          their Member States, of the one part, and the Czech Republic, of the other
          part, *OJ* L360, 31 December 1994.
Europe Agreement Establishing an Association between the European Communities and
          their Member States, of the one part, and the Republic of Estonia, of the
          other part, *OJ* L68, 9 March 1998.
Europe Agreement Establishing an Association between the European Communities and
          their Member States, of the one part, and the Republic of Hungary, of the
          other part, *OJ* L347, 31 December 1993.
Europe Agreement Establishing an Association between the European Communities and
          their Member States, of the one part, and the Republic of Latvia, of the
          other part, *OJ* L26, 2 February 1998.
Europe Agreement Establishing an Association between the European Communities and
          their Member States, of the one part, and the Republic of Lithuania, of the
          other part, *OJ* L51, 20 February 1998.
Europe Agreement Establishing an Association between the European Communities and
          their Member States, of the one part, and the Republic of Poland, of the
          other part, *OJ* L348, 31 December 1993.
Europe Agreement Establishing an Association between the European Communities and
          their Member States, of the one part, and Romania, of the other part, *OJ*
          L357, 31 December 1994.
Europe Agreement Establishing an Association between the European Communities and
          their Member States, of the one part, and the Slovak Republic, of the
          other part, *OJ* L359, 31 December 1994.
Europe Agreement Establishing an Association between the European Communities and
          their Member States, acting within the framework of the European Union,
          of the one part, and the Republic of Slovenia, of the other part, *OJ* L51,
          26 February 1999.
Hänsch, K.
     1992   'The Structure and Strategy for the European Union with Regard to its
              Enlargement and the Creation of a Europe-Wide Order', *European
              Parliament Session Document*, A3-189/92, 21 May.
Maltese EC Directorate
     1990   *Report to the Prime Minister and Minister of Foreign Affairs Regarding
              Malta's Membership of the European Community*, Department of
              Information, Valletta, 22 January.
Okrent, R.
     1958   'Memorandum from the European Economic Community', in *Nego-
              tiations for a European Free Trade Area: Documents Relating to the
              Negotiations from July, 1956, to December 1958*, Cmnd. 641 (London:
              HMSO, 1959): 97-103.
Prag, D.
     1988   'Report on Malta and its Relationship with the European Community',
              European Parliament Session Document, A2-0128/88, 29 June.

Secondary Sources

Adamiec, J.
1993   *East-Central Europe and the European Community: A Polish Perspective* (RIIA Discussion Papers, 47; London: RIIA).

Akagül, D.
1987   'Association CEE-Turquie: A la recherche d'une nouvelle dynamique', *Revue du Marché commun* 303: 3-13.
1998   'Le cinquième élargissement de l'Union européenne et la question de la candidature turque: la fin d'un cycle, mais quelle perspectives?', *Revue du Marché commun et de l'Union européenne* 419: 359-69.

Ananiadès, L.C.
1967   *L'association aux Communautés européennes* (Paris: Libraire Générale de Droit de Jurisprudence).

Balkir, C.
1993   'Turkey and the European Community: Foreign Trade and Direct Foreign Investment in the 1980s', in C. Balkir and A.M. Williams (eds.), *Turkey and Europe* (London: Pinter): 100-39.

Becker, J.
1983   'Artikel 238 [Assoziierungsabkommen]', in H. von der Groeben *et al.*, *Kommentar zum EWG-Vertrag* (Baden-Baden: Nomos Verlagsgesellschaft, 3rd edn).

Bonde, A.
1998   A New EU Debate just around the Corner?, Norwegian Ministry of Foreign Affairs, Oslo, November (via http://odin.dep.no/ud/nornytt/ua-099.html).

Buck, K.H.
1978   *Griechenland und die Europäische Gemeinschaft: Erwartung und Probleme eines Beitritts* (Bonn: Europa Union Verlag).

Coufoudakis, V.
1977   'The European Economic Community and the "Freezing" of the Greek Association, 1967–74', *Journal of Common Market Studies* 16.2: 114-31.

Dienes-Oehm, E.
1996   'Institutional Connections', in F. Mádl and P.-C. Müler-Graff (eds.), *Hungary: From Europe Agreement to a Member Status in the European Union* (Baden-Baden: Nomos Verlagsgesellschaft): 85-90.

Euraconsult
1991   *Cyprus and the European Community* (Nicosia: Euraconsult).

Eisl, G.
1997   'Relations with Central and Eastern European Countries in Justice and Home Affairs: Deficits and Options', *European Foreign Affairs Review* 2.3: 351-66.

Evans, A.
1997   'Voluntary Harmonisation in Integration between the European Community and Eastern Europe', *European Law Review* 22.3: 201-20.

Flaesch-Mougin, C.
1980   *Les accords externes de la CEE: essai d'une typologie* (Brussels: Editions de l'Université de Bruxelles).

Gowan, P.
1993   *EU Policy towards the Visegrad States* (London: UNL Press).
Grabbe, H., and K. Hughes
1998   *Enlarging the EU Eastwards* (London: Pinter/RIIA).
Gstöhl, S.
1997   'Successfully Squaring the Circle: Liechtenstein's Membership of the
            Swiss and European Economic Area', in M.O. Hösli and A. Saether
            (eds.), *Free Trade Agreements and Customs Unions: Experiences, Chal-*
            lenges and Constraints (Maastricht: EIPA): 163-76.
Handtke, C.
1995   *The Europe Agreement with Hungary* (Baden-Baden: Nomos Verlags-
            gesellschaft).
Henig, S.
1971   *External Relations of the European Community: Associations and Trade*
            Agreements (London: Chatham House).
Hitiris, T.
1972   *Trade Effects of Economic Association with the Common Market: The*
            Case of Greece (New York: Praeger).
Ilkin, S.
1990   'A History of Turkey's Association with the European Community', in A.
            Evin and G. Denton (eds.), *Turkey and the EC* (Opladen: Leske and
            Budrich): 35-49.
Inotai, A.
1994   'Central and Eastern Europe', in C.R. Henning *et al.* (eds.), *Reviving the*
            European Union (Washington DC: Institute for International Economics):
            139-64.
Kennedy, D., and D.E. Webb
1990   'Integration: Eastern Europe and the European Economic Communities',
            Columbia Journal of Transnational Law 28.3: 633-75.
Keskin, Y.
1979   'The Turkey–EEC Association and its Problems', in W. Gumpel (ed.),
            Die Türkei auf dem Weg in die EG: Möglichkeiten und Probleme einer
            Vollmitgliedschaft in der Europäischen Gemeinschaft (Munich: Olden-
            bourg): 65-72.
Khol, A.
1985   'Im Dreisprung nach Europa: Kooperation-Assoziation-Union', *Euro-*
            päische Rundschau 13.3: 29-45.
Kinass, J.
1979   *The Politics of Association in Europe* (Frankfurt-am-Main: Campus).
Kiss, T.
1995   'Prospects of the Political Dialogue after the Copenhagen Summit: A
            Hungarian Perspective', in B. Lippert and H. Schneider (eds.), *Monitor-*
            ing Association and Beyond: The European Union and the Visegrád
            States (Bonn: Europa Union): 275-84.
Kramer, H.
1988   *Die Europäische Gemeinschaft und die Türkei: Entwicklung, Probleme*
            und Perspektiven einer schwierigen Partnerschaft (Baden-Baden: Nomos
            Verlagsgesellschaft).

Kramer, H.
1996   'The EU–Turkey Customs Union: Economic Integration amidst Political
            Turmoil', *Mediterranean Politics* 1.1: 60-75.

Krenzler, H.G.
1992   'Der Europäische Wirtschaftsraum als Teil einer gesamteuropäischen
            Architektur', *Integration* 15.2: 61-71.

Kronenberger, V.
1996   'Does the EFTA Court Interpret the EEA Agreement as if it were the EC
            Treaty? Some Questions Raised by the Restamark Judgment', *Interna-
            tional and Comparative Law Quarterly* 45.1: 198-211.

Lindberg, L.N.
1963   *The Political Dynamics of European Economic Integration* (Stanford:
            Stanford University Press).

Lippert, B.
1990   'Etappen der EG-Osteuropapolitik: Distanz-Kooperation-Assoziierung',
            Integration 13.3: 110-25.

Lippert, B., and P. Becker
1998   'Structured Dialogue Revisited: The EU's Politics of Inclusion and
            Exclusion', *European Foreign Affairs Review* 3.3: 341-65.

Lippert, B., and H. Schneider (eds.)
1995   *Monitoring Association and Beyond: The European Union and the
            Visegrád States* (Bonn: Europa Union).

Luchaire, F.
1975   'L'association à la Communauté économique européenne: Perspectives
            d'avenir', *Revue juridique et politique: indépendence et cooperation* 29.4:
            422-35.

Lycourgos, C.
1989   *L'association de Chypre à la CEE* (Paris: Presses Universitaires de
            France).
1994   *L'association avec union douanière: un mode de relations entre la C.E.E.
            et des Etats tiers* (Paris: Presses Universitaires de France).

MacLeod, I. *et al.*
1996   *The External Relations of the European Communities: A Manual of Law
            and Practice* (Oxford: Clarendon Press).

Martonyi, J.
1996   'The Role and Impact of the Association', in F. Mádl and P.-C. Müller-
            Graff (eds.), *Hungary: From Europe Agreement to a Member Status in
            the European Union* (Baden-Baden: Nomos Verlagsgesellschaft): 25-30.

Mastropasqua, C., and V. Rolli
1994   'Industrial Countries' Protectionism with Respect to Eastern Europe: The
            Impact of the Association Agreements Concluded with the EC on the
            Exports of Poland, Czechoslovakia and Hungary', *The World Economy*
            17.2: 151-69.

Mayhew, A.
1998   *Recreating Europe: The European Union's Policy towards Central and
            Eastern Europe* (Cambridge: Cambridge University Press).

McGoldrick, D.
1997   *International Relations Law of the European Union* (London: Longman).

Messerlin, P.A.
1992   'The Association Agreements between the EC and Central Europe: Trade Liberalization vs Constitutional Failure?', in J. Flemming and J.M.C. Rollo (eds.), *Trade Payments and Adjustment in Central and Eastern Europe* (London: RIIA/EBRD): 111-43.

Mitsos, A.G.J.
1983   'Greece: The Industrial Sector', in J.L. Sampedro and J.A. Payno (eds.), *The Enlargement of the European Community* (London: Macmillan): 105-27.

Müller-Graff, P.-C.
1997   'Legal Framework for Relations between the European Union and Central and Eastern Europe: General Aspects', in M. Maresceau (ed.), *Enlarging the European Union: Relations between the EU and Central and Eastern Europe* (London: Longman): 27-40.

Müller-Graff, P.-C. (ed.)
1997   *East-Central Europe and the European Union: From Europe Agreements to Member Status* (Baden-Baden: Nomos Verlagsgesellschaft).

Nielsen, I.
1979   'A View from Inside', in L. Tsoukalis (ed.), *Greece and the European Community* (Farnborough: Saxon House): 13-16.

Norberg, S.
1992   'The Agreement on a European Economic Area', *Common Market Law Review* 29.6: 1171-98.

Oppermann, T.
1962   'Die Assoziierung Griechenlands mit der Europäischen Wirtschaftsgemeinschaft', *Zeitschrift für ausländisches und öffentliches Recht und Völkerrecht* 22.3: 486-508.

Pedersen, T.
1990   'EC–EFTA Relations in the European State System', in F. Laursen (ed.), *EFTA and the EC: Implications of 1992* (Maastricht: EIPA): 71-83.

Peers, S.
1995   'An Ever Closer Waiting Room?: The Case for Eastern European Accession to the European Economic Area', *Common Market Law Review* 32.1: 187-213.

Penrose, T.
1981   'Is Turkish Membership Economically Feasible?', in D. Rustow and T. Penrose, *The Mediterranean Challenge. V. Turkey and the Community* (University of Sussex: Sussex Research Centre): 41-118.

Perdikis, N.
1981   'Greece and the EEC', *Peuples méditerranéens/Mediterranean Peoples* 15: 101-26.
1986   'An Assessment of Cyprus' Association with the EEC', *Journal of Economic Science* 13.2: 38-51.

Plessow, U.
1967   'Was ist Assoziation gemäß Artikel 238 EWG-Vertrag?', *Österreichische Zeitschrift für Außenpolitik* 7.3: 183-97.

Pomfret, R.

1982 'Protectionism and Preference in the European Community's Mediterranean Policy', *The World Today* 38.2: 60-65.

1986 *Mediterranean Policy of the European Community: A Study of Discrimination in Trade* (Basingstoke: Macmillan).

Redmond, J.

1993 *The Next Mediterranean Enlargement of the European Community: Turkey, Cyprus and Malta?* (Dartmouth: Aldershot).

Redmond, J. (ed.)

1997 *The 1995 Enlargement of the European Union* (Ashgate: Aldershot).

Rey, J.

1963 'L'association de la grèce et de la turquie à la C.E.E.', *Annuaire européen/European Yearbook* 11.1: 50-58.

Rollo, J., and A. Smith

1993 'The Political Economy of Eastern Europe's Trade with the European Community: Why So Sensitive?', *Economic Policy* 16: 139-81.

Rossi, E.

1986 *Malta on the Brink: From Western Democracy to Libyan Satellite* (London: Institute for European Defence and Strategic Studies/Alliance Publishers).

Roucounas, E.J.

1964 'La politique commune dans la CEE et association avec la Grèce', *Revue hellenique du droit international* 17.1-2: 25-49.

Saclé, A.

1968 'L'association dans le Traité de Rome', *Revue trimestrielle de droit européen* 4.1: 1-18.

Schwok, R.

1992 'The European Free Trade Association: Revival or Collapse?', in J. Redmond (ed.), *The External Dimension of the European Community: The International Response to 1992* (Basingstoke: Macmillan): 55-76.

Steinbach, U.

1977 'Auf dem Wege nach Europa? Die Beziehungen zwischen der Türkei und der Europäischen Gemeinschaft durchlaufen eine kritische Phase', *Orient* 18.1: 79-101.

Sverdrup, U.

1998 'Norway: An Adaptive Non-Member', in K. Hanf and B. Soetendorp (eds.), *Adapting to European Integration: Small States and the European Union* (London: Longman): 149-66.

Toledano Laredo, A.

1992 'The EEA Agreement: An Overall View', *Common Market Law Review* 29.6: 1199-1213.

Toulemon, R.

1967 'L'association à la Communauté économique européenne est-elle une formelle d'avenir?', *Revue du Marché commun* 100: 145-50.

Tsalicoglou, I.S.

1995 *Negotiating for Entry: The Accession of Greece to the European Community* (Dartmouth: Aldershot).

Tsardanidis, C.
    1984   'The EC–Cyprus Agreement: Ten Years of a Troubled Relationship, 1973–1983', *Journal of Common Market Studies* 22.4: 114-31.
    1988   *The Politics of the EEC–Cyprus Association Agreement 1972–82* (Nicosia: Publications of the Social Research Council).

Tsoukalis, L.
    1981   *The European Community and its Mediterranean Enlargement* (London: George Allen and Unwin).

Ungerer, W.
    1964   'Die Assoziierungspolitik der EWG', *Aussenpolitik* 15.10: 685-97.

Vali, F.A.
    1971   *Bridge Across the Bosphorous: The Foreign Policy of Turkey* (London: John Hopkins Press).

Weil, G.L.
    1970   *A Foreign Policy for Europe? The External Relations of the European Community* (Bruges: College of Europe).

Weiss, F.
    1992   'The Oporto Agreement on the European Economic Area: A Legal Still Life', *Yearbook of European Law*: 385-431.

Wellenstein, E.
    1979   'Twenty-Five Years of European Community External Relations', *Common Market Law Review* 16.3: 407-23.

Wilson, R.
    1992   *Cyprus and the International Economy* (London: Macmillan).

Winters, L.A.
    1992   'The Europe Agreements: With a Little Help from Our Friends', in *The Association Process: Making it Work: Central Europe and the European Community* (CEPR Occasional Paper, No. 11; London: CEPR): 17-33.
    1993   'Expanding EC Membership and Association Accords: Recent Experience and Future Prospects', in K. Anderson and R. Blackhurst (eds.), *Regional Integration and the Global Trading System* (Hemel Hempstead: Harvester Wheatsheaf): 104-25.

Yannopoulos, G.N.
    1975   *Greece and the European Communities: The First Decade of a Troubled Association* (Beverly Hills: Sage).

General Index

Author Index

UNIVERSITY ASSOCIATION FOR CONTEMPORARY EUROPEAN STUDIES
UACES Secretariat, King's College London, Strand, London WC2R 2LS
Tel: 0171 240 0206 Fax: 0171 836 2350 E-mail: uaces@compuserve.com
http://www.uaces.org/u-info/

UACES

University Association for Contemporary European Studies

THE ASSOCIATION

- Brings together academics involved in researching Europe with representatives of government, industry and the media who are active in European affairs
- Primary organisation for British academics researching the European Union
- Over 500 individual and corporate members from Dept such as Politics, Law, Economics & European Studies, plus a growing number of Graduate Students who join as Associate Members

MEMBERSHIP BENEFITS

- Individual Members eligible for special highly reduced fee for The Journal of Common Market Studies
- Regular Newsletter - events and developments of relevance to members
- Conferences - variety of themes, modestly priced, further reductions for members
- Publications, including the new series *Contemporary European Studies*, from May 1998
- Research Network, and research conference
- Through the European Community Studies Association (ECSA), access to a larger world wide network
- Information Documentation & Resources eg: The Register of Courses in European Studies and the Register of Research into European Integration

Current Cost of Membership per annum - Individual Members - £20.00; Graduate Students £10.00; Corporate Members £40.00 (2 copies of documentation sent and any 2 members of Dept / Organisation eligible to attend conferences at Members' rate)

APPLICATION FOR MEMBERSHIP OF UACES

Please indicate if you wish to receive details of the JCMS ☐

I enclose Banker's Order / cheque for £ _____ payable to UACES

Name _____

Faculty / Dept _____

Institution _____

Address _____

_____

Tel No: _____

Fax No: _____

E-mail: _____

Signature & Date _____

Address for correspondence if different:

_____

_____

BANKER'S ORDER FORM

Please return to UACES and not to your Bank

TO_____(Bank)

_____ (Sort Code)

AT _____(Address)

_____

Please pay to Lloyds Bank (30-00-08), Pall Mall Branch, 3-10 Waterloo Place London SW1Y 4BE

in favour of UACES Account No 3781242

on the _____ day of _____

the sum of £20 (TWENTY POUNDS) and the same sum on the same date each year until countermanded

Signature & Date _____ _____

Account No _____

Name _____

Address _____

_____